ISBN O-9552984-0-7

First published in August 2006

Published by
POD Publications
4, Hill Farm Close
High Halstow
Rochester
Kent
England
ME3 8SS
Ph: 01634 250112

Barman Duffy
"always a gentleman"

In memory of a truly remarkable man who moulded our lives and influenced the lives of so many others. Paddy (Barman) Duffy, a Waterside man, a Derry man and . . . . . always a gentleman.

by
Gavan and Marie Duffy

Acknowledgements

We would like to express our grateful thanks those who have made significant contributions both to the sponsorship behind the production of this book and to the content of the book itself. We are eternally grateful to you all.

Sponsorship

Garvan O'Doherty
Michael Doherty
Frances Corry and Family

Content

Harold Alderman
Eamon Baker
Eddie Campbell
Bishop Edward Daly
James Doherty
Sammy Donaghey
John (Red) Doran
John Ferguson
George Fitzpatrick
Martin Gallagher
Joe Mac Carthy
Andy McClea
Siobhan McEleney (now deceased) via The Derry Journal
Conal McFeely
Mitchel McLaughlin
Frankie McMenamin
Alec O'Donnell
Jimmy (James) A Porter
Yes Publications
Greta Vance
Mark Willett

Very Special Thanks to

Elaine Doherty
Harry Doherty, Chairman of the Kent Ex-Boxers Association
Bernadette Healy
Des Quinn

A Heartfelt Thank You

To all those, too many to mention individually, who have helped, encouraged and supported us throughout our journey. We cannot thank you enough.

Foreword from the Duffy Family

The quotation *"Once a Derry man always a Derry man, once a Waterside man always a gentleman"* was one of Paddy's favourite sayings, invariably used mischievously for the craic to provoke discussion and debate. When we were trying to decide on an appropriate title for the book, "Barman Duffy….. always a gentleman" felt so right.

Since his death in 1996, many people have approached us who were curious to find out more about his life, his interests and his achievements. There has also been a hunger to gain greater insight into Paddy's background, beliefs and experiences that moulded him into the person that he was. We believe he would have been deeply honoured to share his life story with the community that he cared so much about. For these reasons, this book has been written by the Duffy family so that all profits from its sale will be shared with the Foyle Hospice and the Foyleview School. This is what Paddy would have wanted and we are proud to be able to do this in his memory.

It's hard to use ordinary words to summarise the life of a truly extraordinary man. What was it that drove him to achieve what he did, and, why are people interested and inspired by that? Paddy was born the youngest son of a family of six and from an early age demonstrated great musical, artistic and physical talents. He was hired out as a farm hand at the tender age of thirteen and went on to join the Irish Army. He became a professional boxer, bouncer, artist, sculptor, poet, philosopher and family man. He went to Rome to see the works of Michelangelo and by an amazing twist of fate had a private audience with Pope Paul V1. People who knew Paddy would not just marvel at his artistic talents but also the person that he was.

Throughout the book we have included a number of the sayings and verses that Paddy often quoted, some which he wrote himself and some written by others that held special meaning for him. The ones he wrote himself have the initials POD (Padraig O' Dubaigh) associated, and the others are extracted from other authors and sources. We believe that these provide an insight into the beliefs and values that directed and drove him to achieve what he did in his life and may be a source of inspiration to others.

The picture of our immediate family was taken in October 2005. In the front row from the left are Sheila, Sadie and Marie. At the back from the left are Gavan, John and Patrick. Sadie (Paddy's wife, affectionately nicknamed the Big Bird by him) did not want her age to appear in print and that will be respected ...she was however born in August 1918 and yes, Paddy would have said that! Gavan has been the driving force and inspiration behind the entire project to get the book underway. The content itself has been written by Marie (that's me) and I will narrate the story on behalf of the family.

We hope that you will enjoy reading about Paddy's life and that a lot of smiles, memories, tears (not too many) and pride will flow in abundance. Thank you.

1.   *The Opening Round*

"All the flowers of all the tomorrows are in the seeds of today."

POD 1992

The earliest picture of Paddy at eighteen months.

Patrick Benedict (Barman) Duffy was born on 26th March 1920 and entered the world as the youngest of five brothers to John and Elizabeth Duffy. The family was completed a few years later by the arrival of a sister. They initially lived in Violet Street, Waterside and then moved to Prospect House at the bottom of Chapel Road. Daddy used to tell us that the house was a fascinating place for them as children because of its corner position and its odd triangular shape. The house boasted three front doors which confused most visitors and in particular the postman, who delivered post to each of the three house addresses, 2 Chapel Road, 170 Spencer Road or Prospect House. The top floor attics provided a lot of amusement for the Duffy boys in particular as they had great sport teasing their younger sister who, eventually became convinced that the house was haunted.

After a few years the family moved again literally across the road to 163, Spencer Road where they resided until all had grown up and left home. In recent years the house was taken over by an adjacent shop and has now been integrated and converted into Murphy's Chemists.

Paddy's father, John Duffy was a mild, slim man of average height who originally hailed from Dungloe. He worked in Miller Water Company, Murphys and Watts Distillery. John was a deliveryman and his mode of transport was a horse drawn wagon pulled by a lovely working horse called Bob. Bob was a great favourite with the children in the Waterside who would usually muster up a wee treat for him when he passed by on his rounds.

John was a member of the Irish National Foresters (INF), an offshoot of the parent organisation, the Order of Foresters which was set up in England by serfs in the days of the feudal landlords. The rules of the INF were those of the parent body i.e. non-sectarian, non-political with no class distinction.

Paddy's father, John Duffy

The organisation today is defined as a mutual aid society, established to help members in distress and support the relatives of members who have died. In Derry the INF was widely recognised as an organisation that helped and supported ordinary people across the city to save, manage their finances and generally provide a social infrastructure. The Irish National Foresters Headquarters, which was in Magazine Street just around the corner from Butcher Street, was a very grand building previously owned by the Masonic Lodge. We understand that the building itself was demolished in the early 1980's.

Paddy's father,
John Duffy, in the uniform of
the Irish National Foresters

The jacket worn by John in the picture is deep green colour with gold braid around the lapels and gold coloured regalia on the cuffs and epaulettes which are just visible in the photograph. Each button is embossed with the date 1782 and has the name 'Comyns & Son, Dublin' engraved on the back. The jacket itself is still well preserved today, a fitting tribute to the quality of the material and the tailoring of the time.

John died on 23rd May 1943 after a short illness and sadly we didn't get to meet our grandfather. We loved looking at the old pictures of him and even today it is still striking how a lot of men of that era looked very similar in old black and white photographs. Probably the most dominant features being a generous moustache and a cap or hat.

Elizabeth Duffy (nee Sharkey) know to us as Granny Duffy, was a tall, slim lady who had wonderful hands for sewing, knitting, embroidery and crocheting. In her later life, Granny Duffy spent a lot of her time doing intricate handiwork and embroidery on Irish linen which she transformed into alter cloths, table clothes, children's dresses and a host of other wonderful things. She used to fascinate us with the meticulous way she would pull individual warp and weft threads from the material to create delicate features on her creations. Looking back now we can see that Granny Duffy had a great flair for design accompanied by the patience to pay attention to such small detail, a gift which she clearly passed on to her son Paddy and which he exploited throughout his life.

The names of John and Elizabeth's children at birth were rarely the names they were known as throughout their lives. It was a tradition in those days to shorten names, or to replace them with a nickname, usually to denote a unique characteristic of the person, or, to differentiate between people with the same name. The creativity and wit used to generate nicknames was a great source of interest to Paddy and later on in the book we've included his complete collection of Derry nicknames....all 445 of them!

John and Elizabeth's family in order were ; John Francis, known as Johnny. William Gerald known as Willie. Joseph, who was known as Joe, had a twin brother called Patrick who died at around one year old. Then came James who was known as Jimmy. The last

Our grandparents, John and Elizabeth Duffy with their dog in the foreground

of the boys, Patrick Benedict was known as Paddy, Pat and Pappy. Again in a common tradition of the time, Paddy was named after the twin who died. The last member of the direct family and the only girl was Patricia Theresa who was known as Trea.

The family number grew when Elizabeth's sister-in-law died and her children, Willie and Ginny Sharkey joined the family and grew up with them. In those days if a parent died or could not provide for their children, the close family would rally round to do their best to integrate the children into their own families. Orphaned children from large families were often dispersed across a number of relatives to share the load. The consequences otherwise were dire as children who were not old enough to look after themselves or be looked after by close family would be sent to a children's home to be cared for.

School Days

One of Paddy's school friends, James (Jimmy) A Porter, recalls some memories of his school days.

"I remember my early school days in 1925 at the Waterside Boys school and the boys in my class. We were all five years of age.

My best friends and classmates included Jim McGuinness who had the nickname Gindo and Patrick Duffy who we called Pappy. Next door to where I lived at 22 Dungiven Road, Waterside, resided the Hargan family. There were two sons and a daughter. The eldest son was called Patrick but was known by his nickname Hootsie. The other son was Jamesie. The family knew more than I did about my origins as I had been adopted. My nickname I hated. When I was a child, Hootsie nicknamed me Lordy because of the clothes I wore as a baby. A wardrobe of silk and satin clothes came with me to my new home.

I remember the Duffy family very well. They lived at No. 2 Chapel Road and then moved across the road to 163, Spencer Road. When they lived in Chapel Road, my recollection was a talking parrot in a cage on a table inside the front parlour window. The parrot was a great attraction to us children. We would knock on the glass window and the parrot would scold us. This brought Mr Duffy, the father, to the door and he would chase the children away. Paddy and I were in the Waterside Boys Choir. The choir was trained and conducted by the teacher Redmond Friel. We sang at Mass on Sundays. When we had bus trips to Donegal, Paddy usually led the singing on the bus. When there were parish concerts in the St. Pats Hall, Spencer Road, we were always called to do our bit should it be Gilbert & Sullivan operettas or Church Choir recitals.

We were trained to box by Spider Kelly in the basement of St. Pats Hall Boys Club. At that time the boy's school was in Malvern Terrace. The boys were on the ground floor and the girls on the upper floor and never the two should meet.

The Principal of the boy's school was George Deehan. We nicknamed him Shoot because he was not liked and his favourite expression was 'I'll shoot the boots off you.' It was the practice of Shoot to send a boy called Corky Doran to his home in Clooney Terrace every morning at 11am for a special billy-can of hot barley water prepared by his sister. On one occasion Paddy Duffy, Jim McGuinness and two or three pupils and I were ordered to collect a number of seating forms from St. Pats Hall and bring them to the school a distance of a few hundred yards.

We noticed little packets being put into the doorways of houses by the Postman. When we recovered some of these packets they contained six Beecham Pills. We collected as many packets as possible. We then waylaid Corky Doran returning to the school with Shoots barley water. All the Beecham Pills were put into the billy-can. We sat in our class watching Shoot drink the barley water. When he had finished the liquid he would eat up the barley with a long spoon. Shoot was not seen at the school again for a week!"

Daddy used to tell us lots of stories about things that happened to him when he was young just so that we should appreciate and be grateful for what we actually had rather than moan about the things we didn't have. Even though times were really hard for him and his family, he would always find a humorous angle or a positive spin to tell the story. My brother Patrick remembers Daddy telling us about his experience when he made his First Communion.

"Daddy didn't have a suit to wear for his First Communion and so his mother decided that he could try to squeeze into his cousin's suit for the day, there really wasn't any other alternative. His cousin, Willie Sharkey had made his First Communion two years previously and the misfit was obvious from the start. Daddy was much taller and much broader than Willie at that time, even with two years of age difference.

Daddy used to laugh when he would tell us about his First Communion day spent in Willie's very tight trousers; unable to sit down and directing all his energy to keeping his backside and decency intact. To add to the events of the day, he didn't have any shoes and his mother managed to borrow a pair from one of the neighbours. They had to be returned to the owner before the end of the day and fortunately they were a bit big so he had to stuff the toes with old socks to fill the space. He used to remark that it was just as well he was the youngest of five brothers and not sisters otherwise God knows what hand-me-downs he'd have had to wear!

Paddy and his mother shared a very similar sense of humour and mischief and when he came in from school she would always ask him what he did that day. He used to tell us about a particular bit of banter they shared about his endeavours to preserve the life of his boots. Having boots and shoes was a luxury and if anyone was lucky enough to get a pair (usually handed down) they would be well looked after. Paddy used to tie his boot laces together, string them around his neck and would walk barefoot to school in an effort to prolong their life. His mother used to tease him and pretend to tell him off by saying *"don't let me catch you playing billiards with your good boots on"*

It's fascinating and very humbling to hear stories of really hard times and poverty where the threads of humour have been extracted and over time they dominate the memories.

Paddy's sister, Trea was the youngest of the family with five older brothers and recalled a story from her childhood.

> "One lovely summer day all five boys decided they wanted to go for a walk. My mother asked them to take me. I was only about four at the time and insisted on taking my doll and pram. Off we went for the day promising to be back in time for our tea. Teatime came and went and there was no sign of us. Alarm bells started to ring with my mother and father as we were rarely late for meals. They were just about to raise the alarm when they spotted the figures of the five boys in the distance. Anxiety grew again as they couldn't see me and one of the boys was pushing my pram.
>
> Did I get lost, did I have an accident, did someone take me away they thought? Not at all, I was fast asleep inside the dolls pram after a long day on little legs spent with my brothers. When I fell asleep they simply tucked me into the dolls pram with my doll on top and pushed me home for my tea."

At the age of twelve, Paddy sold The Belfast Telegraphs outside the Midland Picture House in the Waterside. During the interval he overheard someone being introduced to the audience and on further enquiry, found out it was Jack Doyle, the Irish Heavyweight Champion boxer who was then tipped to be a future world champion title holder. This was a defining moment for Paddy to see a real boxer who believed he was destined for greater things beyond the hopes and dreams of most ordinary people. This chance exposure to Jack Doyle instilled some early seeds of ambition into Paddy's mind that had some influence on the future direction of his life.

Jack Doyle, an ex-Irish Guardsman was a very colourful character who hailed from Cobh, Co. Cork. He stood six foot five inches tall, weighed around 15 stone and was known as "The Gorgeous Gael." He had great talent both as a boxer and a singer and was renowned for living life to the full. Jack was bought-out of the army by a boxing promoter called Dan Sullivan who spotted his potential and staged his rise to fame throughout the UK.

He literally stormed his way to boxing fame and in July 1933, he fought Jack Petersen in London for the British Heavyweight Title. Although his boxing career to then had been incredibly successful, it was reported that his love of the high life had distracted him and he did most of his preparation for the fight in pubs and hotel bars. Petersen was a powerful and skilful opponent and the attendance at the fight in the White City Stadium numbered 90,000. The fight ended in controversy when Doyle was disqualified in the second round for "an outrageously low blow" and the title went to Petersen.

Jack then decided that his future boxing opportunities lay in the USA and just before he sailed from Cobh on "The Washington" in 1934, he addressed a huge crowd from the balcony of the Atlantic Hotel in Cork. He announced that he would come back with the World Championship and would then marry a sweet Irish colleen. The upshot was that he didn't achieve either. He lost the qualifying fight to Buddy Baer via a knockout in the first round and married a Mexican girl called Maria Louisa Castaneda also known as Movita Castaneda. She was an actress and a singer and went on play the role of the island girl in the 1935 release of Mutiny on the Bounty. When their marriage ended, she married Marlon Brando in June 1960 and that marriage ended in divorce in June 1968.

Sadly Jack died, destitute and alone in St. Mary's Hospital, Paddington, London on 13th December, 1978 at the age of 75. An old friend of Jack's from his heyday brought his remains back to Cork where he had a funeral fit for a king and where "The Gorgeous Gael" is still fondly remembered today.

The Artist Emerges

As a young man, Paddy's hands were always busy. He would scribble and draw on scraps of paper and spend hours whittling on pieces of wood and shaping it with fragments of glass, creating different patterns and textures. In these moments of simple pleasure he was renowned for whistling his favourite tunes. At around thirteen years of age he entered an art competition and drew a Scotsman in a kilt with a long flowing beard. This resulted in the first formal recognition of his talent as an artist and he won first prize from the British Dominion School of Art. The prize consisted of pencils, balloons and leaflets on "How to Draw."

Paddy was also an avid reader and took a great interest in philosophy and poetry, both classical and humorous. The hours of reading and reciting poetry in his younger days no doubt helped to embed the words into his memory. He could still recite many word for word in his later years.

His favourites included "The Lake Isle of Inisfree" and "The Shooting of Dan McGrew." Although school provided a foundation of knowledge and learning, Paddy was very much self-taught and self-motivated to explore the world around him and discover the artistic and literary treasures it contained. He had a particular curiosity about the true meaning behind words and would seek to explore those depths rather than be satisfied with a superficial acceptance of the words themselves. For this reason many people who knew him described him even at a young age as a great thinker and philosopher.

The family home was a very musical place and all the children were taught to play the piano. Paddy himself was a child soprano although as time went by his voice dropped in range significantly and he eventually sang bass. Although he had learned the rudiments of music and sight-reading, he played very much by ear and once he had mentally logged a tune he could play it without the need for sheet music. Paddy's brother, Johnny was a particularly accomplished pianist and won many prizes at the Derry Feis and music festivals. Paddy took special interest in the harmonica and in later life purchased a Hohner 64 Chromatica Professional Model in the key of C which spanned four chromatic octaves – that's what is written on the box! It basically allowed him to play a wide range of tunes in different keys. He always kept the harmonica in its original box where it still remains today.

The Hiring Fair

At thirteen years of age Paddy left school. The school leaving age wasn't recognition of the maturity of thirteen year olds for an adult life; it was purely a reflection of the economic constraints of the education system at that time. He was tall, physically strong and looked older than his years. Times were hard and so Paddy decided that he would hire himself out to get income for the family. He took himself off to the Hiring Fair or "rabble" as it was locally called which took place at The Diamond on the opposite corner from McKinlays Tailors & Clothiers, and Scotts - The Complete House Furnishers. Potential hirelings would go along to the Fairs hoping to be hired by farmers for seasonal work. The hirelings didn't get paid until the end of the season and it was a very tough existence living on the farm and working all the daylight hours.

The Fairs were held twice a year in May and November on three consecutive Wednesdays. On the first Wednesday, the hirelings from the previous season were released and could spend a short time with their families before being rehired on the second Wednesday.

The second Wednesday was the Hiring Fair proper when the new hirelings would be selected by their new paymasters. The third Wednesday was very much a mop-up affair when farmers and potential hirelings who had not been matched up the week before could try to seek suitable arrangements. The Hiring Fairs in Derry stopped around the mid 1930's.

Paddy was hired to a farm in Eglinton where he dug potatoes from dawn til dusk. The accommodation was very basic as was the food. Paddy recalled getting a pot of stews on the Monday and eating from the same pot on the following Saturday. The work was back-breaking and the rewards were few, in fact, Paddy didn't get paid at all for that season's work due to a dispute with the farmer. The going rate was 1/6d (7.5p) for a 12 hour day and for stacking up corn the rate rose to 2/- per day (10p). Much as this was a traumatic experience at the time for a 13 year old, he recalled the memories of the experience with great humour in his later life. We never did find out what the dispute with the farmer was about!

The Origins of Barman

Shortly after leaving school and his experiences as a hireling, Paddy went to work in the Exchange Bar in Joseph Street, just off Rossville Street as a barman........ and yes, that was enough to award him the nickname Barman that stuck with him for the rest of his life. Paddy attributed the coining of his nickname to Joe Doherty, a well known local pole-vaulter of the time and one of his training partners.

Paddy was always fascinated by the origins of nicknames and the processes by which they become common language to identify individuals. He collected a vast number of local nicknames throughout his life and his complete collection of Derry nicknames, is contained in "The Collector" chapter of the book. Your name may be there!

2. *The Soldier*

"When you put your boots on in the morning, you never know who will take them off at night."

Unknown

In early 1939, Paddy went on a weekend trip to Dublin where he met a group of pals who were planning to join the Irish Army. He went along with them to Portobello and joined the Second Field Company General Service Corp on 20th March 1939. He served much of his time at the Columb Barracks, Mullingar. Paddy's primary role was a Motor Transport driver which he combined with representing his command in boxing tournaments both within and outside the army.

Paddy on his recruitment to the Irish Army

In all, Paddy served in the regular army for 2 years and 207 days. On leaving the army, the testimonial contained in his Certificate of Service book completed by the Commanding Officer, reads :

> *"Private P Duffy has been employed in this camp as an MT driver Grade 2 for the past two years. During that time I have found him honest, sober and attentive to his duties. I recommend him for any position his abilities enable him to undertake."*

Some memories of Army days from one of his colleagues, Jimmy (James) Porter.

"On my 20th birthday I enlisted in the Irish Defence Forces. In 1940 I was stationed in Collins Barracks in Dublin. A weekend boxing tournament was arranged between boxers in the Eastern and Western Command. I was surprised and delighted to find that Paddy Duffy was to be one of the contestants from the Western Command. He won his bout. After the tournament we had a concert for the visitors. Paddy had a wonderful singing voice. I will never forget one of the songs he sang, it was "A Nightingale Sang in Berkley Square."

On the Sunday after the boxing tournament, Paddy and I got together and decided to visit O'Connell Street in Dublin. We dressed in civilian clothes. You were always sure to meet Derry people at any time in this street. Sure enough, who did we see walking towards us, none other than Gindo McGuinness. He invited us into his hotel for a coffee. It was the 'An Staid' Hotel in North Fredrick Street, Dublin.

We took our leave from Jim at around 6pm. An hour later many people in the Hotel including Gindo were arrested and interned in the Curragh Interment Camp in Co. Kildare. They were to remain there for the next four years. The Gods smiled on Paddy and me that day. It appears that the hotel was used by the out of town activists and subversives and Paddy and I were extremely lucky to leave the hotel when we did."

Irish Army football team

Paddy can be seen on the far right of the photograph kneeling alongside his pals in the football team. Even at that young age he wore a tabby bow which continued to be his signature dress code throughout his life.

After his regular army service, he then transferred to the Army Reserve where he continued his part-time service for a further 25 years. Paddy was very proud of his army days where he continued to be an active member of the local branch of the Ex-Servicemen's Association and joined in all the annual reunions. It was a fitting tribute to him that the ex-servicemen of the *Oglaigh Naisiunta Na hEireann* formed a guard of honour alongside his tricolour draped coffin on the day of his funeral.

James Doherty, an active member of the Organisation of National Ex-Servicemen for over thirty years reflects on his memories of Paddy.

"Paddy was a man larger than life. In army barracks, language was rarely the choicest. Paddy's was however impeccable. He spoke as a Christian and a gentleman. Despite his great physical strength he would never descend to being a bully.

When incapacitated he sought ways of overcoming his disability – including a lift at the side of the stairs in his home. Paddy was also an avid collector and was always cheery and good-humoured. He was the prefect role model of a patriot."

3. *The Boxer*

"I thought I was poor when I had no shoes, then I saw a man who had no feet on which to put shoes."

Unknown

While Paddy was at school, he and his brothers spent a lot of time at St. Pats Hall in the Waterside keeping fit and picking up the early rudiments of boxing. Early on, he recognised that his build, strength, attitude and athletic skill could help him shape a future in boxing. He had seen a glimpse of Jack Doyle and had been enthused by how an ordinary person from a poor background could develop and exploit a natural talent.

Paddy started boxing competitively as soon as he left school and fought almost every week at the Plaza, a hall behind Fox's Corner (just off Rossville Street on the corner by Barr's Pawn Shop.) He started as a featherweight and over the years matured into a formidable six-foot, fourteen stone, heavyweight professional boxer.

In the early years he fought for a few shillings in local venues and by the late thirties he was earning as much as £30 boxing professionally in Dalymount Park, Dublin, under his own name, and, the exotic name of Larry Esposito. Boxing under assumed names, particularly foreign names, was a standard practice in those days in order to attract the crowds. Although Paddy had dark hair and a fairly dark complexion, he looked the part but had to make sure that he didn't speak in case his accent would give the game away and expose the fact that he wasn't Spanish. Paddy was also often billed as Pat or Patsy Duffy, again a practice used by fight promoters to excite the crowds into believing that there may be new talent on display.

Paddy went on to spend a number of years as a professional boxer moving from the light heavyweight to heavyweight division. Many of his fights took place in the Guildhall in Derry where the support from the local crowd was always a welcome advantage. He also fought extensively at venues in Belfast, Dublin and across England, Scotland and Wales. He used to tell us that the majority of fights at the Guildhall were put on for local entertainment and that there would be some great craic and great characters that made the experience more memorable.

Paddy particularly remembered that well-known local character, Greta Torrens who was an avid boxing supporter and would sit at the front row of the ringside to cheer and encourage local boxers. She would often rise to her feet and go the corner during the interval between the rounds to energetically and noisily spur on the local contender.

Greta Torrens, the accomplished horsewoman

My brother John had some additional memories of Greta.

> "I remember when Daddy used to take us out the town we always wanted to go
> along by Little James Street just across the road from Sackville Street. The
> attraction for us was a really big parrot that was left outside on a perch when
> the weather was good. There was a big sign saying that it could bite but
> that didn't stop us getting close and trying to get it to repeat some thing we
> had said. I have a really clear memory of Greta wearing a tweed trouser suit
> with a shirt and tie and joining in the noisy banter with people who passed by
> the shop. She had a reputation as a 'great horse woman', that's the words I
> remember people using at the time. Greta would always talk about the boxing
> times at The Guildhall and although our attention was usually focused on the
> parrot, it sounded as though they had a great craic."

These photographs of Paddy were taken in 1942 when he was twenty-two years of age. Like many boxers of the day, he wore his initials, PD, on his shorts. Considering the lack of training facilities and to a great extent the lack of in-depth knowledge of fitness, training and nutrition for professional athletes, he developed a wonderful physique coupled with exceptional technical and physical boxing skills.

"Autographed phot of Paddy dated 20/12/1942"

17

*Back Row left to right: Sam Edgar (Masseur), third from left Mickie McMenamin
(Cruiserweight), Joe Quinn from Buncrana (Middleweight),
Paddy Duffy (Heavyweight), Jimmy McVeigh (Trainer):
Middle Row left to right: Jimmy (Spider) Kelly, Willie Fenn (Featherweight),
Dan Doherty (Manager), John (Red) Doran (Lightweight)
Jackie McCallion (Lightweight)
Seated Front: Billy (Spider) Kelly, Gerry McCauley (Featherweight)*

This wonderful photograph was taken in 1947 in a room above the Fire Station in Hawkins Street which was used as a boxing gym. When the Fire Station closed, the gym moved to a stable in William Street.

Sam Edgar (back left) was the masseur and was affectionately known as *"sandpaper hands."* Although the young boxers didn't always relish the rub-down, it was thought very unlucky not to have Sam's sandpaper hands do their business in loosening up the muscles before and after training. There was a certain pride in smelling of olive oil and wintergreen on the way home! Training took place six nights a week for around 90 minutes. The standard training programme was designed to prepare the boxers for the intense energy required to fight in the ring. It comprised a series of planned exercises for three minutes duration with a 60 second rest interval to replicate the three minute bouts in the ring.

Some highlights from Paddy's boxing career :

One of his earliest recorded professional fights was on September 23rd 1942, when he fought against Seaman O'Brien in the Guildhall in Derry in the light-heavyweight class. The armed forces stationed within or close to Derry provided a great opportunity for their aspiring boxers and local boxers to practice their skills and engage in some "healthy competition." It also provided a rich mix of talent and entertainment for the audience who appreciated seeing boxers from "the mainland" perform in local venues. Paddy won the bout as Seaman O'Brien sustained a cut over his eye in the first round and the referee stopped the fight.

On 16th February 1944, Paddy fought Frank Boylan from Belfast in the Guildhall, again in the light heavyweight class. Frank was very well known on the boxing circuit and on this occasion Paddy lost the fight.

The 12th July 1946 was a memorable occasion when Paddy fought Tom Feely from Roscommon in Dalymount Park, Dublin. This was a semi-final heavyweight competition and Paddy won the fight through a knockout in the first round. On the same night, he went on to fight Jack (Red) O'Hara from Dublin in the final and lost on points.

Both boxers had undergone a gruelling schedule as Jack had also fought on the same night beating Jim O'Connor in his semi-final bout.

This picture of Paddy was taken walking along O'Connell St. Dublin the day after the fight with Tom Feely and Jack O'Hara. He had taken a left hook from Jack O'Hara and had a swelling on his right cheek which is just visible in the picture.

Paddy fought Alex Woods from Randalstown on 10th August 1946 in Belfast for the Northern Ireland Heavyweight title and was beaten in the third round on a technical knockout. Alex was a frequent contender for the Northern Ireland Heavyweight title and had a very impressive track record winning most of his bouts by knockout.

The day after . . . .

On 1st November of the same year, Paddy lost on points to Tom Reddington from Salford in Blackburn, England. Tom also had a very impressive record with some of his most prominent opponents being Bruce Woodcock and Jack London. Tom fought Bruce in March 1944 and was knocked out in the second round. Bruce Woodcock was one of the most formidable heavyweight boxers of his era who gained many titles including : the British Empire Heavyweight Champion, Commonwealth (British Empire) Heavyweight, European (EBU) Heavyweight. Bruce won most of his fights through KO (Knockout) or TKO (Technical Knockout) with some of his most eminent opponents being Jack London and Joe Baski.

The Bruce Woodcock Connection

Bruce Woodcock also fought Martin Thornton from Spiddal who was nicknamed the "Connemara Crusher." In the film "The Quiet Man" starring John Wayne, Martin Thornton played John Wayne's stunt double in some of the fight scenes.

Bruce had previously beaten Jack London in July of 1945 for the British Commonwealth Heavyweight title. Jack London, who was also known as John George

BRUCE WOODCOCK

Autographed photo of Bruce Woodcock

Harper, held an amazing fight record from 1931 to 1949 with 95 recorded wins, 52 of them by knockout.

Bruce was so impressed by Paddy's style, attitude and skill that he asked him to spar with him in Doncaster in preparation for his British Heavyweight Empire title fight. Paddy at that time was working in the Gas Yard and he was granted six weeks leave by his manager, Mr Walmsley, to join Bruce as his sparring partner to help him prepare for the title fight. Bruce went on to win the title. Mr Walmsley was originally from Doncaster, the same hometown as Bruce Woodcock and was very proud to release Paddy for the fight preparation. For his sparring role, Paddy was paid £40 per week which at that time was "big money" and significantly more than he would have ever earned on the boxing circuit or working in the Gas Yard. Paddy and Bruce were regularly seen running around Doncaster Racecourse in the early mornings as part of their training.

Although Bruce continued to fight competitively, he did not make a full recovery from the severe jaw injuries he sustained from his fight with the American, Joe Baski. His last recorded fight was in November 1950 when he lost to Jack Gardner fighting for the British Empire Heavyweight Title. Bruce died in Doncaster, England in December 1997.

Lee Savold, Jack Solomons and Bruce Woodcock

The foremost promoter in the history of British boxing, Jack Solomons brought top American fighters to England in the post-World War II period, when boxing enthusiasm in that country was at its peak. Solomons spent close to 50 years in the sport during which he staged 26 title fights.

Born into a family of fish marketers, Solomons first import to Britain was live carp. He became involved in boxing in the 1930s as the manager of Eric Boon and as operator of the Devonshire Club, a boxing venue for up-and-coming London talent. He also worked as a matchmaker for the leading promoters before venturing into his own shows. His first big promotion was the Bruce Woodcock-Jack London British heavyweight title fight.

In 1946, when he brought American world light heavyweight champion Gus Lesnevich to England to face Freddie Mills, he opened the door to many more transatlantic matches.

A connection with the famous Mike Jacobs, then the pre-eminent American promoter, helped to provide Solomons with the best American talent. Solomons quickly became the most important man in British boxing. He had the best fighters, and he created an air of theatrical excitement around his fights that greatly advanced the sport's popularity. The Sugar Ray Robinson-Randy Turpin middleweight title fight in 1951 was perhaps Solomons most memorable production. The programme cover for this bout didn't show the fighters, but rather featured a large photograph of Solomons himself in an extrovert pose, wearing his classic bow-tie and smoking an enormous cigar.

Competition and the growth of television gradually reduced Solomons influence, but he continued to stage many important bouts until his death in 1979. He brought Muhammad Ali (then known as Cassius Clay) to England in 1963 to fight Henry Cooper, and he opened the private World Sporting Club and staged many promotions through its auspices.

Lee Savold was one such boxer brought to Britain by Jack Solomons. Savold hailed from Marshall, Minnesota and had a total of 133 recorded fights. He won 88 fights overall, 64 of them by knockout. Toward the end of his boxing career, Savold fought Joe Louis in June 1951, in Madison Square Gardens, New York and was knocked out in the 6th round. His last recorded fight was with Rocky Marciano in February 1952 in Philadelphia, when he lost in the 6th round to a technical knockout.

Paddy Duffy and Joe Louis - Two Degrees of Separation

On 2nd June 1947, Paddy fought the very talented Jamaican boxer, Charlie Brown in Swansea (recorded in The Boxing News June 11th 1947). Paddy lost when the referee stopped the fight in the third round of a ten round bout. Brown was nicknamed the "Jamaican Carnera" and was likened to the famous Primo Carnera who won the World Heavyweight title in June 1933. Brown fought with the initials JC – Jamaican Carnera, embossed on his trunks. Primo Carnera fought the world famous Joe Louis, also known as the "Brown Bomber", in June 1935 and lost by a technical knockout.

The following report about Charlie Brown was written in The Boxing News, March 17th 1948.

> *"Two minutes were all that Charlie Brown, Jamaica (14st. 4lb) required to knock out Charlie Collett, Hemel Hempstead (14st. 11lb) in an eight rounds bout at Welwyn Garden City on March 10th. Brown, who had been acting as **sparring partner to Joe Louis,** landed a straight right to the solar plexus before either had had a chance to sum up his opponent and before many of the spectators had settled down."*

Two degrees of separation between the Irish boxer and his ultimate boxing hero.

Charlie Brown
(Jamaican Carnena)

The boxer whom Paddy admired most was Joe Louis. He believed that the combination of the hand skills of Joe Louis and the light-footed technique of Sugar Ray Robinson was the ultimate recipe for success, the recipe that developed into Mohammed Ali.

Paddy admired "gentleman fighters" who focused on skill to outwit their opponent and not brutality to hurt or maim them. He didn't have, and didn't aspire to have, the "killer instinct", he was by choice a tactician who operated with respect and integrity and not by raw brute force.

Andy McClea recalls some poignant and enduring memories of Paddy.

"Way back in the 1940's I used to train for the City of Derry Harriers and was interested to experiment with some boxing training. I used to watch Barman training….. from a distance and hoped that he would notice me. I was really in awe of him and as a wee boy of nine stone, I was just over the moon when he took me under his wing and showed me a few moves to help me achieve my goals. I always remember that his stomach muscles were like a brick wall and that was one of the things I too wanted to achieve. He had a great physique.

I have never heard anyone, not anyone, ever say a bad word about Barman. He was the absolute gentleman and would always help people out. Barman gained his reputation for the person he was inside. He was a great philosopher and I loved to listen to him, not just his advice on boxing but his views on the world and life in general.

Years later I used to literally go out of my way to find him when he would be sketching around William Street and Rossville Street just to catch up with him and share in a bit of banter. He made a really lasting impression on me and I will never, ever forget him."

Daddy used to tell us about the joys, trials and tribulations of his boxing days and how boxers had to provide and maintain their own kit, more often than not borrow some of the basics down to the gloves and boots. Advertisements from the Boxing News in September 1949 record the cost of some of the components of a basic boxing kit. Although we may smile at the costs when translated into today's currency, in those times it was an additional overhead for aspiring boxers and often a barrier to them being able to develop their skills.

24

Paddy with famous Derry boxer, Jimmy (Spider) Kelly

Jimmy Kelly and his son Billy, who were both nicknamed Spider, were the first to hold a unique father and son boxing record. They both held the same title, the British Empire Featherweight Title. Jimmy won the title in 1938 when he beat Benny Caplan in the Kings Hall, Belfast and Billy beat Sammy McCarthy in the same venue in 1955. A similar father and son record was held later by Jack and Brian London who both held the British Empire Heavyweight Title.

I recently met young Spider (Billy) in Derry and spent a few hours with him soaking up his experiences of his boxing days. During the conversation he said that his nose had only been broken once. Was is a big fight, was it when he was sparring . . . . no, it was when he was playing with his pals and fell over in the street cracking his nose on the edge of the pad!

4.   *The Bouncer*

"A man's not drunk who from the floor can rise again and call for more but drunk is he who prostrate lies and cannot either call or rise."

Unknown

In 1941 Paddy returned from his service in the Irish Army. He secured a full time job in the Gas Yard, officially called the Londonderry Gaslight Company and also began working in the Corinthian Ballroom as a bouncer five nights a week. During and after the Second World War, Derry was an important naval base. The influx of off-duty sailors looking for entertainment in the city promoted the demand and growth for dances virtually every night of the week. In 1941, it was estimated that there were 20,000 sailors from all nationalities based in Derry. Unlike today, alcohol was not available inside the dance halls and equally, people were not allowed into the dances if there were any indications that they had consumed more alcohol than they could sensibly manage.

Despite the vigilance of the bouncers, fights frequently broke out and the main role of the bouncers was to defuse the situation and enable everyone to continue to enjoy their night out. The following story is recalled from an interview with Paddy and appeared in Fingerpost, Artist's Notebook in the Winter 1987 edition :

> *"One particular New Year's night in 1947 'all species of soldiers, sailors and service men' became embroiled in rows throughout the evening. Barman and Mickie Mc Menamin (a fellow bouncer) noticed that present at each row was a particular sailor who always protested his innocence. The two bouncers resolved to put an end to the fights. They gave the sailor the 'Coup De Grace' down the stairs and then went up and cleared a circle in the middle of the dance floor declaring that anyone wishing to fight should step forward and 'fight man to man'. There were no further fights that night!"*

Martin Gallagher provided the following story recalled by his father Billy Gallagher, now deceased:

> *" During the war Barman was a bouncer at the Corinthian. The doors had been shut but a group of sailors kept kicking them, screaming that they wanted in. The doormen were fed up with all the noise and it looked as if the sailors would succeed in breaking the doors down. Barman told all the onlookers from the dance who had come down to gawk, to go back up the stairs and told one of the other doormen to open the door and that he would quickly run past him up the stairs.*

The doorman did that and the four sailors, who were all big men, sauntered in with smiles on their faces. Barman was halfway up the stairs when one of the sailors shouted up to him that he had better get out of the way as they were coming up. Unperturbed, Barman said, 'come on up and better still, anyone that gets past me can get in for free.'

The four of them bolted up the stairs at him and needless to say. . . . no one got in free. Minutes later, with a lot of persuasion and a minimum of force, they were all peacefully deposited outside the door with diplomacy ruling the day. My father said that Barman only ever used force when all else failed and was a true gentleman."

Paddy's diplomacy and tact in handling difficult situations and his sense of fairness and gentleness in dealing with people was very widely recognised. Despite his physical strength and athletic abilities, he always chose to try to dispel anger in others through discussion and negotiation rather than by resorting to physical violence. He hated to see people get hurt through irrational behaviour fuelled most often by too much alcohol. One of his tactics when he spotted someone who may be heading for trouble or picking fights with other revellers, was to try to appeal to their respect for their parents and head them off before they got in too deep. He would often say *"What would your mother say if she saw you in that state?"* or, *"If you carry on behaving like this somebody's going to break your nose and what will you poor mother say when she sees you in hospital?"* One of the beliefs that he both lived and worked by was:

> "Never attribute to malice what can adequately be explained by stupidity"
>
> Unknown

Paddy's services as a bouncer were in great demand and he worked at many venues across and outside the city including The Guildhall, The Corinthian, Borderland, The Stardust and the Boat House in Coleraine.

The Corinthian Ballroom * Alcohol was not allowed to be brought in

We've not been able to trace the identity of everyone in the photograph. Paddy is on the far right and we know that the lady on the far left was Miss Lecky whose father owned the Corinthian ballroom. The sign in the background may be hard to decipher but it did spell out the basic rules for entry

Pictured Left: A group of bouncers taken at a function at the Guildhall, Derry. From left: Paddy, Brian Breslin, John Ferguson, John McGeady, Tony McIntyre and Liam Begley

* No pass-outs (i.e. people were not allowed to come in and out again on the same ticket)

Pictured Right: Taken at Borderland, in 1966, Paddy in the middle with John Ferguson on left and Brian Breslin on right

* Anyone under the influence of alcohol would be asked to leave

28

Taken at the Stardust (Cameo) a group of young bouncers learning their craft from John Ferguson and Paddy. From left: Sammy Holden (deceased), Liam McSwine, Willie Taggart, Jimmy Kelly (back), Gerry Taggart (front) (deceased), John Ferguson, Paddy McSwine (deceased), Paddy Duffy, Gavan Duffy and Patsy Loughrey

Some memories of the dance hall days from Mitchel McLaughlin

"The world was a more innocent place in the 1960's even though hugely important events were occurring. The US was doing its worst in Vietnam and Cambodia and the Israelis had just annexed huge swathes of Palestinian territory after the six-day war. Dylan, the Beatles and the Rolling Stones were revolutionising music and George Best was working his magic on the soccer field. Barman Duffy, as he had done for years was keeping the peace in Borderland although it was becoming apparent that the heyday of dance halls was coming to an end.

Kathleen looked stunning. She was dressed in a white woollen dress and I thought I was in love. Well actually I was in love, with my new car! Well it wasn't a new car either; it was my first car, A Ford Anglia, which cost me £105 in Desmonds Garage. I waited until the last dance and asked Kathleen if I could take her home, mentioning that I had my car with me. It was how it was done in those days and it was a definite plus if you had your own 'wheels'. She said 'Aye.'

Kathleen collected her coat and we headed for the car. Barman Duffy wished us a goodnight and safe home. Not that he knew either of us, Barman wished everybody leaving the dance hall a safe journey and he meant it.

So far so good I thought.... quick snog at the side of the Squealing Pig, back to the car, home to Derry, a fish supper at "The Celtic" and then sit in the car outside Kathleen's house until her Da would shout at us.

But the bloody car wouldn't start! I was a learner driver and had flooded the engine. I have hated petrol engines ever since. Kathleen offered to help, but I couldn't see how she could manage it if I couldn't. (Well I didn't know then what a male chauvinist I was.)

Eventually I gave in when it became obvious that I wasn't going to get as much as a cough out of the engine and the Borderland bus had long departed. Needless to say Kathleen managed to start the treacherous car almost immediately and to my chagrin then drove me home. In my own car! It took me days to get over it and years to talk about it!

But a fortnight later, I tried again. I called up to Kathleen's house and she agreed to a date and we arranged to go to Borderland that weekend. I was improving at my driving and even the car was behaving. Happy days! Friday night, Borderland and the Miami Showband, I was anticipating a night to remember. I didn't know how right I was!

I had managed to drive all the way without stalling once and we arrived at the dancehall. The crowd was in boisterous form and it promised to be a brilliant night. Barman was there at the pay kiosk as usual, keeping order. He greeted everybody as usual and we all queued more or less patiently. Kathleen was ahead of me in the queue and just as I was about to pay for our tickets there was a sudden commotion from the entrance of the hall!

I looked up to see a man come rushing through the double doors of the hall. He was charging at me. Or so I thought. I still don't know why, but I lashed out and struck him and knocked him to the floor. Pandemonium, a near riot developed as friend and foe took sides.

Barman stepped in and grabbed me by the back of the neck and helped the young man to his feet. Another doorman arrived and explained what had happened inside the hall. It seems the fella had mistakenly walked into the Ladies and then fled the scene in embarrassed confusion. I had completely misread the situation.

Barman shook his head, and with a gentle (but massive) hand on the back of my neck showed me out to the street. I thought there was a chance that he might have done more than that but he was as professional as ever. He obviously understood that I had made a stupid mistake and was prepared to give me a fool's pardon. 'I wouldn't come back for a week or two if I was you' was all that he said. Kathleen looked at me as if she had never seen me before in her life and paid her own way into the dance.

'Bounced' out of the dance by Barman, dumped by Kathleen, I could do no other than 'home alone' again. I got into the car, it started first time, the only thing that went to plan that night."

5. The Family Man

"Once a Derry man always a Derry man, once a Waterside man, always a gentleman."

POD

When Paddy Met Sadie

In 1948, Paddy was introduced to Sadie Smith by one of his workmates from the Gas Yard, Billy McFeely. Sadie lived with her mother, Fanny (Frances) Smith in 105, Lecky Road which was around 200 yards from the Gas Yard entrance.

Fanny Smith (nee McFadden) and her husband Charles were both born in 1877 and were married in St Eugene's Cathedral. Sadie was the youngest surviving child of the Smith family and was preceded by Eddie (Edward), James, Charlie (Charles), Hugh and Cess (Frances). Sadie (Sarah) had a younger sister Kathleen, who died when she was six weeks old.

Sadie at age 18

An amazing twist to the tale of Paddy and Sadie meeting emerged through their first conversation. In typical Derry fashion, the early conversation when people meet for the first time explores their background and ancestry with "Who's your granny" type of questions. Paddy proudly announced that he was from Spencer Road in the Waterside and Sadie asked if he knew her "Uncle" John Duffy who also lived in Spencer Road. After further exploration in trying to locate her Uncle John, Sadie remarked that John Duffy wasn't actually her uncle but was a friend of the family. It transpired after a further few rounds of questions that "Uncle" John Duffy was in fact Paddy's father.

The real twist to the tale is that when Paddy's father, John Duffy and Sadie's mother, Fanny Mc Fadden were young, they were engaged to be married. Fanny broke off the engagement on friendly terms when she met Charles Smith and they went on to marry. John remained in contact with Fanny, Charles and the family for many years and was awarded the title of "Uncle John" by Sadie. Sadly he died in 1943 after a short illness. It was only through the process of writing this book that this piece of local knowledge emerged and although not earth shattering in itself, it caused our minds to spin with some "what if" scenarios….*"if our mother's mother had married our father's father, would we be here today?"* Mind boggling!

Paddy would often joke and say:

> *"I came over from the Waterside one night for my tea and never got out again – she put handcuffs and a strait jacket on me."*

On Saint Patrick's Day in 1949, Paddy and Sadie got engaged to be married. They celebrated their engagement by going to Buncrana for the day on a Lough Swilly bus.

Sadie recalls,

> *"It was a really nice day and we decided to go to Buncrana. I'd bought a lovely new rig with a hat that had a plume of feathers to one side – I thought I was lovely! We walked along the shore and it got a bit windy so we went and had some lunch. After our lunch we went back to the shore while we were waiting for the bus and would you believe it 'a giant seagull came along and s**t right on top of the feathers of my new hat.' I was disgusted and had to carry my hat all the way home - I never did wear it again. What a waste of a good hat!"*

Sadie and Paddy on their engagement day, 17th March, 1949

The insult to the hat wasn't made any better by Paddy who tried to keep a straight face and explain that the seagull probably recognised the feathers on her hat as those of one of its distant relatives and that "its message" was a sign of luck for the future. That didn't wash....nor did the hat!

The Waterside Man Moves to the West

Paddy and Sadie made a very handsome couple when they were married at the Long Tower chapel on 1st August 1951, a memorable date as it was also Sadie's birthday. The wedding actually took place at 7am! Sadie was so nervous about the wedding that Father McMonagle agreed to marry them at that time to help her overcome her nerves on the day. Sadie's mother was at home preparing the wedding breakfast for the group and by 9.30am, Paddy and Sadie were on board the train to Dublin for their honeymoon.

Paddy & Sadie on their wedding day -1st August 1951.

Wedding Party front from left :Trea Duffy (Paddy's sister), Paddy, Sadie and Hugh Smith (Sadie's brother)
Middle row from left : Jimmy Duffy (Paddy's brother), Elizabeth Duffy (Paddy's mother),
Annie Duffy (wife of Paddy's brother Willie), LaLa Kelly (family friend) and Willie Duffy (Paddy's brother)
Back row : Bridget Duffy (wife of Paddy's brother Jimmy), Bridget Lynch (sister of Willie's wife)
and Sarah Maguire (family friend.)

In those days it was traditional for the wedding party to escort the newly married couple on the way to their honeymoon. Paddy & Sadie are pictured with their wedding party at the Great Northern Railways (GNR) station in Foyle Street to start their honeymoon journey to Dublin.

The wedding party at the GNR station

35

Paddy & Sadie on their honeymoon in Dublin in 1951

Sadie still has a receipt for the two-tier wedding cake, which cost £5.10d. In the tradition of the times, the top layer of the wedding cake was stored in an airtight tin with an apple and was eaten the following year at the christening of their first child, Marie. By all accounts it was perfectly preserved and tasted just as good as it did on the wedding day. Paddy and Sadie continued to live in the Lecky Road where they raised their family of five, Marie, Gavan, Sheila, Patrick and John.

Receipt for wedding cake

The family home in the Lecky Road was always full of pets, waifs and strays. Paddy loved dogs and would frequently take in strays or dogs which were under threat of "being taken away by the man" i.e. being put to sleep if they couldn't be found a home. One such beast was an Irish wolfhound called Bran who ate everything in sight. Bran could easily reach the clothesline and managed to eat a series of nappies, my rag doll and many other items, which dangled within his reach. Probably the most remarkable feast that Bran consumed was Paddy's field and track running shoes - with metal spikes. Bran ate the entire leather uppers and made the wise decision to leave the spikes.

Paddy loved all animals and had a particular affection for smooth haired fox terriers. Throughout his life he could be seen with a white and tan fox terrier called Pedro. There were in fact three consecutive Pedros who all looked amazingly similar. Paddy got his fox terriers from a breeder out the Lecky Road, Bob Matthewson who was also a shoemaker. Bob bred the champion fox terrier "Brow o' the Hill" and Paddy's fox terriers came from the same bloodline. Paddy got Pedro No. Three as a twelve week old puppy on 21st February 1986.

Did You Kiss Your Granny?
Every Sunday, Daddy would take us to see our Granny Duffy in the Waterside. All five of us would trek with him from the Lecky Road, up to The Diamond, along Carlisle Road, across Craigavon bridge and then along Spencer Road to number 163. If we were lucky, we would approach the Bridge just as a steam train would be passing below either entering or leaving the Great Northern Railway (GNR) station in Foyle Street. There was a rare delight in the sight and smell of the steam trains and we used to race each other to be the first to get consumed by the smoke as it drifted across the Bridge. We're still not sure why we did that but it was fun at the time!

Daddy was very particular about appearance and posture, particularly as we were all tall. He was really tenacious about a few "rules" which were close to his heart and which he frequently reinforced with us :

* Never walk along with your hands in your pockets

* Never chew gum in the street

* Never use bad language

* Always walk upright with your head high and your shoulders back

* Always kiss your granny!

Granny Duffy was invariably sitting in the corner of the dining room with a crocheted blanket over her legs and a knitted shawl across her shoulders. She was a very tall lady with long limbs and long nimble fingers. She loved to sew, knit, crochet and embroider and passed some of these skills to her grandchildren, Leah, Sheila and myself. We were fascinated by her skill and dexterity in creating wonderful garments from raw materials. She played the Jew's Harp and we used to beg her to play for us. We can't remember any specific tunes but we do remember dancing around the dining room playing musical chairs while she provided the musical accompaniment. This usually resulted in noisy chaos with us all landing in a heap trying to claim the last chair while she no doubt tried to time the stoppage points to minimise the risk to life and limb – ours that was! We never really did get the gist of playing musical chairs in that all we ever did was reduce the number of chairs but we all remained in the game…I think she knew that and played along with us.

When it was time to leave for the trek back to the Lecky Road, there was a ritual "kissing your Granny" session which Daddy supervised. Each of us in turn had to kiss Granny Duffy goodbye. For Patrick and John who were the smallest, they had the longest journey to climb onto Granny Duffy's knee to kiss her goodbye. Daddy would ask each of us the same question "Did you kiss your Granny?" and if he didn't see the kiss take place, we were sent back for another journey onto Granny Duffy's lap making sure this time to attract his attention so that he could see the kiss in action. We learned that timing was a critical factor as well as being seen to do the right thing. The common cry was *"Daddy, Daddy I'm kissing my Granny,"* a fond memory of an old tradition that we still talk about today and smile.

Rolf Harris Has a Lot to Answer For!
When Daddy first introduced the Stylophone to us at home it was initially quite a novelty, however......it soon became a real source of contention.

What is a stylophone?
For those who may not know or remember, a stylophone was a miniature electronic musical instrument invented in 1967. It was operated by a 9 volt battery and consisted of a metal keyboard, which was played by running a metal stylus along it. The stylophone was popularly known as "the electronic organ in your pocket" and was promoted by none other than Rolf Harris.

For those who may like a technical explanation of its workings, each note was connected to a voltage-controlled oscillator via a different-value resistor – thus closing the circuit and creating a sound. Our description of the sound it created was much more explicit :

"A horrible, buzzy pulse wave through a small cheap speaker that sounded like a burst bagpipe invaded by a gang of angry wasps."

The moral of the story was that Paddy found the stylophone a real source of fun and enjoyment, a sentiment that was not shared with the rest of the family. He would diligently learn to play a host of different tunes and then insist on us listening to them both while he practised and then when they were performed for visitors. We finally resorted to sabotage in order to get some peace and adopted tactics like removing the batteries, hiding the stylus and on one occasion – it got "accidentally dropped." The sabotage plan backfired however when he bought a new stylophone, a larger model with a louder speaker. Gavan even bought him a set of headphones so that he could practice in silence but he refused to take the bait or the hint! This however only resulted in another failed plan so we had to resort to more devious measures.

The process of writing this book unearthed some of the memories that had remained dormant for a few years. We started to ask *"What did happen to the stylophone?"* After a few searches in places where we could have hidden it, the stylophone emerged from the darkest corner of the coal shed – we all blame my brother Gavan for putting it there! A good stylophone never dies – ironically with the addition of a fresh battery, the stylophone burst into life and reconfirmed our original sentiments. It still sounds like : "A horrible, buzzy pulse wave through a small cheap speaker that sounds like a burst bagpipe invaded by a gang of angry wasps."

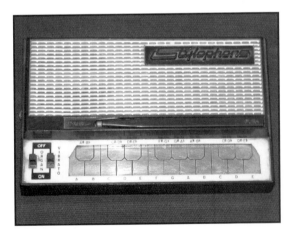

The stylophone, we thought we'd killed it but it lived to play again

Hot Under the Collar

Paddy smoking one of his pipes

Paddy had a wonderful sense of humour and loved puzzles, quizzes and enigmas that needed profound thinking skills to solve. He also had a great ability to laugh at himself......eventually. We fondly recall the story of his misfortune one cold winter's evening when he was working in Campbell's Bar in Duke Street.

It was a very wet and inhospitable evening and he set off to walk to the Bar wrapped up in a sports jacket and overcoat for the cold journey across the bridge. Paddy had carved a number of pipes and occasionally enjoyed a smoke. That night the warm vapours were very welcome in warding off the cold air. On reaching the Bar, Paddy extinguished the smouldering tobacco and tipped out the contents into a drain along the kerb (or so he thought). He put the pipe into the top pocket of his sports jacket and removed both the sports jacket and topcoat together and put them on a coat hook in the staff rest room behind the bar.

It had been a very busy night in the bar and the staff didn't have time to go to the restroom for a break. Four hours later when Paddy opened the restroom door, he found it engulfed in smoke and raised the alarm with the staff. They finally identified the source of the smoke as the top pocket of Paddy's sports jacket. There had obviously been some smouldering ash left in the pipe when Paddy put it into his pocket and it managed to burn an enormous hole through the sports jacket and the top coat over the left hand side of the chest sections of both. The damage was so extensive that the entire left-hand side of both coats were only held together by the collar infrastructure – literally by threads.

Thankfully no other damage was caused that night, it was a lucky escape. However, it was even colder and wetter for the journey home and Paddy had little choice but to wear the burned out coats held together by threads around the collar for his walk to the Lecky Road. Even though he may have felt like "Steptoe" that night on the journey home, he followed his own rules. He walked with his head held high, shoulders back, no chewing gum, didn't use bad language and certainly no hands in his pockets!

The tale of "Paddy the Arsonist" was one we laughed about so many times. The thing that really cracked us up about the whole story was that in the first instance, he blamed the pipe for not going out.....bad pipe..... Secondly, he couldn't accept that the coats were damaged beyond repair and persisted with his mourning for them with the famous

The final *thread* was that he wouldn't allow the coats to be thrown away and hid them away until Mum decided that she didn't want the house looking like "Nellie Ramsays" and threw them out on the day the dustmen collected the bins so that there would be no way back for them (Nellie Ramsay's was a second-hand/junk shop that used to be in William Street. It was a really dark, dingy, smelly, chaotic place which had clothes, furniture, ornaments and objects of all description literally strewn all over the place.) Happy days.

Brandyballs, Jub-Jubes and Nicky Cakes!

It has been amazing the memories that have resurfaced once we started to look back at the things we did as a family. My sister Sheila remembers a particular occasion when a bag of sweets caused chaos in the City Picture House.

"Daddy took us to the matinee one Saturday afternoon to see 'Darby O'Gill and the Little People .' Yes......it was a very long time ago! It was the 1959 version starring a very young Sean Connery. Going to the pictures was always a great treat and part of the ritual was going into a wee shop in Rossville Street on the way to stock up with sweets before going around the corner to the City Picture House in William Street. Our favourite sweets were Brandyballs (balls of hard, sugary, crisp, toffee), Jap Deserts (coconut squares covered with icing), Jube-Jubes (small fruit gums a bit like the fruit pastilles) and Whoppers. Whoppers were like a small chocolate log which cost 1d each. They were always advertised as having "six bites to a bar." We could however demolish a Whopper in two, or sometimes one bite so the advertising wasn't very accurate at all.

We were all lined up along one row in the Picture House and Daddy started passing the bag of Brandyballs along to each of us. It could be that we were entranced with the film but somehow or other, the whole bag of Brandyballs got dropped and started rattling and clattering along the floor of the cinema right down to the front row. For those who may not remember the City Picture House, the seating area was on a really steep slope with no carpet or sound-proofing on the floor, just bare boards.

We were in hysterics because we had lost our bag of sweets and all the children in front of us were ecstatic because they had Brandyballs rattling down on top of them. The noise and chaos was phenomenal, a mixture of the Brandyballs bouncing and thudding along the floor, us crying for our sweets and everyone in front of us whooping with delight at their free sweets. Where's the justice in that?

41

The only compensation we could think of was that when we got home, there would be Nicky Cakes on the table for our tea."

Just in case anyone may be interested in the "Darby O'Gill and the Little People" film or want an overview of the plot, the summary available on the internet goes as follows:

"In the enchanted Emerald Isle, Darby O'Gill spins tall tales of leprechauns and banshees. Unfortunately, when he actually captures the leprechaun king and discovers their hidden gold, no one will believe him!"

What Happened to Nicky Cakes?

For some strange reason we all remember Nicky Cakes. We're not sure just how the name was actually spelled or what the packet looked like. They were really big, thick, round biscuits with holes in the top. They were really crunchy and very dry unless of course they were covered in butter which was the best way to have them. We remember buying them from Danny Quigley's shop in St. Columbs Wells but can't remember where else they were sold. We always associated Nicky Cakes with being on the table for our tea when we came back from the matinee and it was something we really looked forward to. Where did they go?

6.   The Working Man

> "One machine can do the work of fifty men. No machine can do the
> work of one extraordinary man."
>
> Unknown

Paddy joined the Gas Yard in 1941 following his Army service and when he got
married in 1951, he moved to 105, Lecky Road, literally a few hundred yards along the
street so getting to work on time was never a problem. The original Gas Yard or, the
Londonderry Gaslight Company to give it its full title, opened in Foyle Street in 1829
and moved to the site at the corner of the Lecky Road and Stanleys Walk in 1865.

For anyone who lived close by there was no mistaking the unique "eggy" smell and the
heaviness of the air full of black dust and grit. Gavan and myself were often charged
with delivering tea and fresh buns to Daddy while he was at work.

My brother Gavan still has some crystal clear memories of those days;

*"I remember when I was about seven or eight, Marie and myself used to take
regular trips up to the Gas Yard when Daddy was on shifts. My mum used to
make tea and pour it into a milk bottle which had a teaspoon suspended inside
it. When she was sure that the bottle wouldn't break, she took out the teaspoon
and used a cork to seal the milk bottle to keep in some of the heat. We would
walk up the Gas Yard armed with the bottle of tea, sandwiches and freshly
buttered buns.*

*Daddy used to work on the furnaces which were to the left just inside the main
gate. We used to walk straight into the furnace area and would look around in
the dingy light to find out which furnace he was working on. We'd usually find
him by one of the massive fires shovelling in coal or stoking it to remove the
coke. It was as hot as hell in there and Daddy used to open the furnace door so
that we could see the flames and feel the blast of hot air that burst out. I
remember he always had burns on his hands and the hairs on his hands, arms
and eyebrows were always singed."*

I remember an occasion which could have been more serious at the time but which
caused a lot of laughter when it turned out to be all right.

*"On one of our visits to deliver the ritual tea and sandwiches, I remember
Daddy opening up the furnace door and some red hot cinders flew out and
spread across the floor. Gavan and myself jumped back out of the way and
Daddy started shovelling in more coal, which was lying in big piles on the
floor.*

The next thing I saw was that one of the cinders had caught the hem of his trousers alight and was smouldering. I screamed out 'Daddy, your trousers are on fire' and he started jumping around like a lunatic. Thankfully he managed to extinguish the flames and no damage was done......... except perhaps to his pride as the story remained a future teasing-point when we would ask him to show us his Irish dancing skills as demonstrated on that day. Feet of Flames or what!"

People who worked on shifts, particularly where they finished early in the morning, were often asked to "knock up" i.e. knock on the doors or windows of people who had to rise for work as part of their wake up call. If you were awake in the early hours in the Lecky Road you could hear a chain of muffled noises and words move along the street;

"Wake up Paddy, it's half six."
"Half six Mrs McDonough, Bernadette's bus leaves in a half hour."

"The Gas Yard"   *the smoke and the smell*

My cousin, Leah Duffy developed croup when she was around six years of age. It was a really common childhood ailment at the time. She remembered her mother bringing her to the Gas Yard and Daddy walking her around the perimeter of the site a few times so that she could inhale the gasses and vapours which were believed to have therapeutic qualities in curing all sorts of ailments affecting the chest, sinuses, skin and a host of other complaints as well. This was a very common practice of the day and many children and adults made their pilgrimage to the Gas Yard to seek a "cure" by inhaling the fumes created by the combustion of coal as part of the process of producing town gas. An alternative "cure" which would not seem as attractive to a small child, was to be passed under the belly of a donkey three times!

The Gas Yard was certainly a smelly, dirty place for those who worked there and for those who lived in the surrounding environment. Despite that, it helped provide the vital fuel for people across the city to keep warm and get on with their everyday lives.

In our house in the Lecky Road, the Gas Meter was in the hall and had to be fed by 1d (less that .5p) coins to release the gas. We also had a gas iron.....yes a gas iron. The older houses didn't have 13 amp sockets so we didn't have an electric iron until 1971. The gas iron was really unpredictable. There was a gas tap in the kitchen and the iron was attached to it by a flexible tube. When the gas was turned on we had to light a small cavity inside the body of the iron which then heated the ironing plate at the bottom. It was almost impossible to control the temperature and a lot of clothes and school uniforms didn't survive the experience.

Where people didn't have coal or coke fires, particularly in bedrooms, it was really common for paraffin heaters to be used. Mc Laughlin's Coal Shed in the Lecky Road sold pink paraffin which was poured into large glass bottles which had a metal clamp around the middle and a handle which allowed the bottle to be inverted and put into the heater. The paraffin would then be regulated by turning a knob to control the drips that landed on the heated element. It produced a unique but not unpleasant smell and sadly there were many accidental fires and injuries caused if the heater was knocked over or the flow of paraffin wasn't properly regulated.

When we used to go up to the Gas Yard we were always curious about how coke was made from coal and how come it didn't all get burned up in the big furnaces. Daddy used to explain to us about coal being a fossil fuel i.e. created through thousands and millions of years of decomposition of plants and trees that got buried deep inside the earth. The turf (peat) that is extracted from the bogs across Ireland is a precursor of coal and if peat were to be allowed to dry, in a few million years it could evolve into coal.

He went on to explain that coal was composed of a number of chemical compounds, and in order to extract the gas for use as town gas, it was heated up to very high temperatures in the big furnaces he looked after but it wasn't burned. Part of his job was to ensure that the furnaces operated at the right temperature and with the right amount of oxygen to extract the gas, known as "town gas" and enable the residue, coke, to be reused as heating fuel. Sulphur and ammonia, two of the chemicals produced by the gas production process, were considered to have therapeutic affects on people who had chest or skin problems, hence why so many people made their pilgrimages to the Gas Yard seeking a "cure" for their ailments.

The gasometers were massive holding tanks for the gas. The more gas that was produced, the higher the level of the gasometer.

The processing of coal in the Gas Yard produced a substance called coke – not coca-cola or the trendy term for cocaine! Coke was a really efficient reusable fuel as all the gasses had been removed (to produce the town gas) and it produced little or no smoke when it was burned to heat the homes of people across the city. It was cheaper and cleaner than coal and to get it direct from the Gas Yard reduced the cost even more. That's partly why it was a really popular fuel of the time.

The Gasometers and the new plant

46

The Gasometers (Empty)

The Gasometers (Full)
47

The old boiler house

Queuing for Coke

This wonderful photograph was taken in October of 1947 and shows people queuing outside the entrance of the Gas Yard to collect bags of coke. Paddy can be seen on the far left minding the door. People used to queue with their prams, makeshift carts and sack bags to carry the coke back to their homes. Old women or people with mobility problems were ushered to the front of the queue and although the coke was scarce and rationed, the atmosphere was always a good-natured affair bordering on a social gathering. One of the really striking features of the photograph is the happy, eager expressions on the faces. Who are these people and where are they now?

Greta Vance shared some memories of Paddy from her time in the Londonderry Gaslight Company :

> *"I first met Paddy when I worked in the office of the Londonderry Gaslight Company in The Diamond between 1973 – 1982. Paddy, as we called him, came up from the plant and of the Gas Yard in the Lecky Road with the employees' timesheets. He was very likeable telling us a wee joke or some tit-bit of news he had just heard. This is how I remember Paddy."*

Sammy Donaghey worked alongside Paddy in the Gas Yard for many years and recalled some of his memories from his home in Canada.

"What can one say about the legend Paddy 'Barman' Duffy? My name is Sammy Donaghey, friend and workmate of the gentle giant.

My first encounter with him was many years ago. I will not forget the day I went to the Gas Yard for an interview for a job. As I entered the Gas Yard gate, feeling a little nervous, the first person I saw was a giant of a man who immediately spoke to me. I told him I was there for a job interview and he directed me to the office, but I didn't know at that time that I was face to face with the 'Barman' himself.

Over the years we became friends as he had lots of interests that I had myself; everything from coin collecting to sports. He always gave me support in my weight-lifting days. He would say to me 'Sammy, you only get out what you put into it.' Paddy always had the words to help you in any situation. He could talk on any subject; he missed his vocation – I think he should have been a politician.

I left for Canada in the 60's and did not return for 25 years. When I did visit Derry, I made sure that I had a visit with the man himself. I brought him a few coins much to his delight. Each time I returned I made sure I went to see Paddy 'Barman' Duffy – a real Irish gentleman and most of all a great family man and friend.

Thank you Paddy for letting me into a small part of your colourful life."

7.   *The Sculptor*

"Creativity is...seeing something that doesn't exist already and bringing it to life."

Unknown

From a very early age Paddy was fascinated by creating shapes from odd bits of wood and using the natural grain and textures to create different effects and finishes. As a child he would be frequently seen paring an old stick into a recognisable shape while whistling away to his hearts content. Paddy was entirely self-taught and he developed his craft with the simplest of tools; a selection of penknives; a few chisels; sand paper and various bits of glass with differently angled edges for finishing delicate areas.

He first became interested in carving when he saw an old man carving shapes into a potato. Paddy asked him what he was doing and he replied that he was practising his carving skills. He gave Paddy some early advice that held him in good stead.

My sister Sheila remembers Daddy telling her what the old man said :
> *"Always practice your carving first on spuds. Never carve a good piece of wood until you know what you want to do and know that you can do it. Anything that's cut out of the spud goes into the pot so nothing's wasted. If you do that Son, you won't make too many mistakes."*

It is absolutely remarkable in today's world to comprehend how a person can use their imagination and ingenuity to create such intricate and complex works of art without any form of training or tuition. There were no laser cutting tools or computer aided drawing packages to create a perfect design template as is available nowadays. Everything Paddy carved was created by his own hands without the use of machinery or technology. Paddy used his eye for shape and symmetry to design and create the basic layout. He preferred to use scraps of real wood that may have started life in other guises e.g. wooden banisters, old furniture, snooker cues, Christmas trees but to mention a few of his resources. He drew the outline design on the wood in pencil to develop the perspective and balance of the subject and then began the painstaking process of slowly and steadily, cutting and shaping.

There are various theories and schools of thought around the impact of formal education and training on innovation and creativity. Some argue that formalised training narrows and reduces scope for broad thinking while others argue that it provides the stimulus and direction for innovation and creativity to grow. What we do know is that Paddy created his own journey and developed his own route map along the way.

He loved to create the effect of clear space around the central subjects of some of his carvings and these complex and intricate designs can be clearly seen in the selection of pieces shown. For anyone who has never tried to carve anything in wood, it would be very easy to underestimate the difficulty and finality of each cut. There is no going back. When a cut is made it cannot be removed or undone. We remember occasional mishaps when a delicate piece would break and Daddy's response, after an amount of "tutting" was always the same "That was hard lines, I know now what I did wrong and I'll get it right next time." Invariably he did.

We've included a selection of some of Daddy's carvings which we hope will provide an insight into both his creativity and talent.

The Walking Sticks

* This amazing shot provides a view of the complexity of the carvings themselves and also provides clues to the origin of the materials used.
* The second stick from the left was made from a discarded Christmas tree and shows the intricate detail of two intertwined snakes with the space between hollowed out. This was carved entirely from one tree trunk and demonstrates one of the spatial effects that Paddy loved to create.
* The third stick from the left is made from blackthorn extracted from the wild bushes found in Ballyliffin.
* The stick on the far right started life as a snooker cue.

The Walking Sticks
A different perspective to highlight the detail

53

The Walking Sticks

The sticks were not merely decorative pieces, they were practical, usable walking sticks and in later life Paddy would be frequently seen walking with his stick, with a sketchpad in his hand and a dog by his side.

The Walking Sticks

A sample of the many walking sticks that Paddy carved from a variety of materials mostly found and rescued from diverse previous guises.

Smoking Heads
A different perspective to highlight some of the detail and unique features of each pipe.

Smoking Heads
Paddy carved this selection of pipes again from all sorts of odds and ends of wood. The pipes were real in that they could be smoked and Paddy could be seen smoking his favourite pipes while drawing and carving. The various faces and expressions on the pipe bowls provide a clue to Paddy's mischievous sense of humour.

The Devil and the Detail!
A wonderful close up of the mischievous devil face on one of Paddy's pipes.

Is My Head on Fire?
The intriguing facial expression on one of Paddy's pipes.

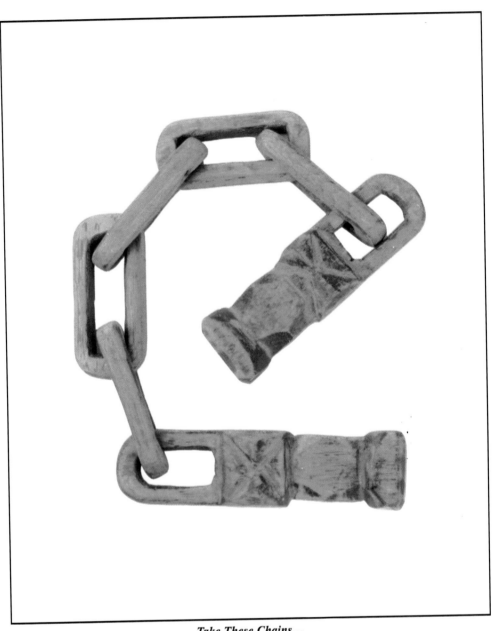

Take These Chains…

Paddy carved a number of chains from a continuous piece of wood and would fascinate even the most sceptical observers about how it was done. He would pose the question "How do you lengthen a piece of wood by cutting it yet keeping it intact? The complexity of what he achieved in this piece is really difficult to describe to do it justice. He started out with one piece of wood of a finite length and through carving the interlocking links in the chain without breaking the length of the wood, the overall length of the wood would be increased. Creating these chains from a solid piece of wood was a massive feat of patience, ingenuity and creative excellence.

Take These Chains...

To put this into perspective, the original piece of wood was 11 inches long and with the links outstretched, it is now 13 inches long.

The Guildhall
Carving of the Guildhall from Shipquay Street with Shipquay Gate in the foreground.

The Guildhall
Taken from the Derry walls overlooking the main entrance of the Guildhall. The Guildhall was fondly embedded in Paddy's memory as a place where he had boxed as a young man, where he had worked as a bouncer and where he had enjoyed many plays and concerts.

An Artists Impression
A plaque Paddy created for the local art club showing the skeleton from the City of Derry Coat of Arms in an artists pose in the forefront

Rough Seas

This piece captures the ingenuity and complexity of carving a vibrant image using various depths of cuts to create the motion and intensity of the scene. To the bottom right of the carving the water is relatively close to the surface of the wood and by comparison, the lighthouse in the background required significant excavation to create the sense of distance.

Limerick Lace

A wall plaque showing the full body and head shot of the famous Irish horse Limerick Lace. The Irish Defence Forces Equitation School was formed in early 1926 and one of the first recruits was Ged O'Dwyer of Limerick. Ged rode Limerick Lace to win the Irish Individual Grand Prix five times in 1932, 1934, 1936, 1938 and 1939.

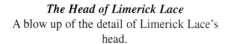

The Head of Limerick Lace
A blow up of the detail of Limerick Lace's head.

The Universal Cross
Paddy designed this piece around the theme of a universal God facing all corners of the world. There is a carving on each aspect and all are joined together in a single theme. The original wood came from an old oak banister.

Pope John XXlll
Paddy carved this piece shortly after the death of Pope John XXlll.

The Rosary

This piece is carved from one piece of wood and the intricacy of creating the space around the hands is quite remarkable. The piece is a reflection of Paddy's religious beliefs and the unity that the rosary portrayed for him.

The Doves of Peace

A symbolic piece with three doves intertwined in a circle, which emphasised Paddy's beliefs in striving for peaceful solutions to conflicts.

The complexity of this piece is not entirely obvious at first sight. The green background is actually a baize backing and the outline of the doves has been carved right through the wood again to create the free space. The amount of patience and attention to detail required to create this work is extremely hard to envisage and Paddy managed to achieve that with his active mind, manual dexterity and simple tools.

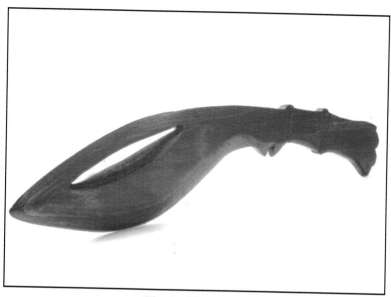

The Gurkha Knife
Although this is carved from wood, it does have a real cutting edge!

Bowls Trophy
This piece was initially designed as a pipe and then Paddy converted it into a bowling trophy for the Pilots Row Bowls Club.

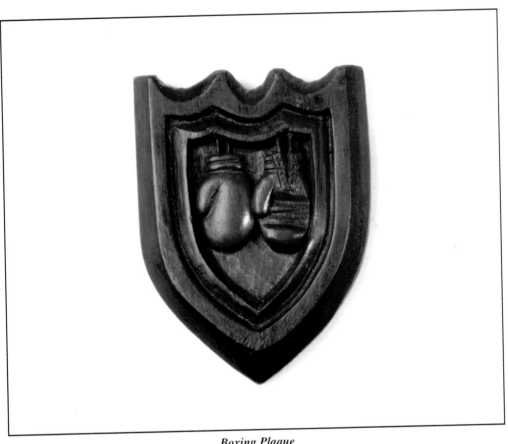

Boxing Plaque
A bit of nostalgia for Paddy creating a simple memento of his boxing days.

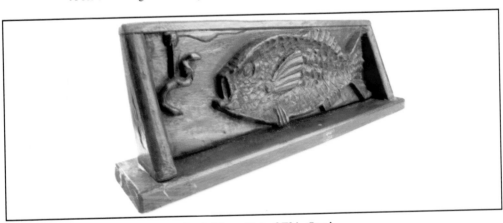

Can't Worm Out of This One!
A detailed piece in oak carved from the remnants of an old sideboard.

Head of Jesus

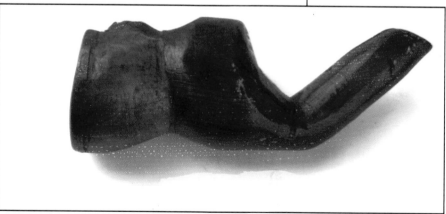

Horses Hoof Pipe
In this piece Paddy demonstrates how a creative mind can turn a piece of wood into a
horse's hoof and in turn create a useable pipe.

66

The Unfinished Work…..

The last piece Paddy started to carve but wasn't able to finish. It's a commemoration plaque he designed for the Irish Army ex-servicemen for a future reunion.

The Unfinished Work…..

He was recreating the emblem on the badge (as in 1 above) as the focal point of the plaque. The rough carvings of the decorative edges are still in outline and a scroll effect drawn in pencil may be seen at the top of the plaque. Unfortunately Paddy developed severe arthritis in his wrists and was unable to finish the job he started.

8. *The Artist and Poet*

"Art is a collaboration between God and the artist, and the less the artist does the better."

Andre Gide

In the late 1950's Paddy and his great friend Willie Golden began to sketch areas of Derry which they thought were likely to be demolished. Paddy described Willie as

"A great character, a shoemaker who would be asked to mend anything from a fishing rod to a mandolin. A very clever man who would sit up all night translating, reading and writing."

They had an enduring friendship and shared many happy hours together sketching, solving puzzles and generally talking in riddles amidst peals of

Pictured left: Paddy sitting amongst the rubble capturing the remains of a Derry landscape

laughter. One of their favourite catch-phrases was : *"Did you hear any more word about thon?"*

Paddy and Willie were both active members of the Derry Art Club and frequently displayed their works at local exhibitions.

Pictured right: Paddy pictured here sketching in the Bull Park, with his dog rory by his side

Paddy in the midst of the Bogside Fleadh with Pedro the Second

A sketch in motion

Paddy can be spotted on the bottom left corner of the photograph with his sketchpad in hand. The white gable on the middle right side of the photograph is the actual monument that we would now recognise as Free Derry Corner.

Vinny Coyle, a great character of his time.

In 1971 we all moved house to Lisfannon Park and Paddy captured in this sketch the early erection of what became affectionately known as "Fort Lisfannon." The sketch was drawn in 1977 and shows the beginnings of a boundary wall being built around the home of a popular figure in Lisfannon Park, Vinny Coyle. Vinny was an extrovert, charismatic character and he and Paddy were often mistaken for each other as they were around the same height, build, age and shared a similar dress sense. Probably the most differentiating characteristic was Vinny's generous handlebar moustache. He is sadly missed as one of the great characters of his time.

Fort Lisfannon

We've included a selection of sketches from various locations across the city. Paddy signed most of his sketches with the initials POD on the bottom right corner to record his name in Irish, Padraig O'Dubaigh. Most of the sketches were drawn with ordinary lead pencil and black biro.

The earliest drawing in the sketchpad of a tugboat at the wooden wharf Derry Quay drawn in 1966. At that time the Quay would have been fully operational and the tugboats were the lifeline of the large boats and vessels to get them safely docked and their cargo unloaded and reloaded. The "Scotch Boat" as it was known journeyed between Derry and Glasgow and was one of the regular features on the Derry Quay landscape. Derry Quay itself was also designated as a "Point of Departure" for those emigrating from Ireland to destinations described locally as "out foreign."

Duke Street, Waterside drawn in August 1968. This was one of the areas where Paddy and his brothers played when they were children. Little did he know that a few months later on 5th October, it would be the focal point for the first Civil Rights March in the city.

The Lecky Road in 1968 showing Quinn's Chemist and the All Cash Stores with the imposing statue of Governor Walker towering over the backdrop. To local people, Quinn's Chemist was much more of a walk-in surgery where all types of ailments and injuries were treated on the premises.

Drawn in 1969 just before it was demolished, a sketch of Barney Coyle's Corner Bar in the Lecky Road at the bottom of Stanleys Walk. The sketch was drawn from Fosters Terrace just opposite the Gas Yard entrance.

73

A view from Meenan Park in 1969 when it was being constructed with the Lecky Road in the lower background. The backs of the houses in Nailor's Row and Friel's Terrace can be seen along the bottom of the Derry Walls in the upper part of the drawing. The Memorial Hall and the base of the Governor Walker pillar can also be seen in the background.

A sketch drawn in 1969 from Paddy's front door at 105, Lecky Road, looking into the recently constructed Meenan Park with Dove House visible on the right hand side.

The Stone Jug and Crana Bridge, Buncrana, drawn in 1976

The Last of Fulton Place.
28-7-76

The last of Fulton Place off Howard Street by the Long Tower Chapel, drawn in July 1976 before its demolition.

The Long Tower Chapel 1977 drawn from Friel's Terrace.
It was the place where Paddy & Sadie got married and where each of the family were christened.

A view of Foyle Street in 1980. This is now the site of Iceland and The Foyleside shopping centre.

George's Bar in Outer Bishop Street drawn in 1980.
The bar itself still stands today but has been renamed.

A view of the entrance to Pennyburn Chapel drawn on 16th July 1981. There is
a bit more to the sketch than is immediately obvious as the vehicle on the bottom
right is a funeral hearse. Paddy recorded in the notes by the side of the sketch
that it was Mrs Deveney's funeral.

77

Tillie & Henderson shirt factory at the end of Craigavon Bridge and the junction of Foyle Street, Carlisle Road and Abercorn Road drawn in 1981. The building itself has since been demolished and the symbolic "Hands Across the Divide" monument created by Maurice Harron now stands in the centre of the small roundabout.

An unusual view of Austins of The Diamond in the background seen from the corner of Foyle Street and Orchard Street drawn in 1981.

Foyle Street in 1981 drawn from the site of the Old City Hotel which was located across the road from the Guildhall.

Drawn in May of 1981, this sketch captures McCorkell's Mill which stood between Queens Quay and the Strand Road. This is now the site of the new City Hotel. The River Foyle would run to the right of the picture.

St. Eugene's Cathedral in 1983 drawn from the Bull Park.

The Marlborough Steps drawn from the corner of the Bull Park looking up toward Marlborough Terrace and Beechwood Avenue. The pillar with the stone on top is said to be a "fairy seat" and it would bring bad luck if it were to be moved.

80

This sketch of Paddy appeared for many years on the mural inside the Richmond Centre. It was drawn by Tim Webster and shows Paddy with one of his faithful dogs, Rory. In his right hand Paddy can be seen using one of the sticks he carved and in his left hand, he's seen holding one of his pipes.

81

Governor Walker's dominance

Paddy had a very agile mind and could see the wit and wisdom in many of the everyday happenings across the city. The imposing statue of Governor Walker reigned in a dominant position on the Derry Walls since it was erected in 1826 and had become a symbol of some of the political and religious divisions across the city.

This great photograph really demonstrates the imposing dominance that had been a common feature of the landscape until August 1973 when it was blown up. Paddy described the occasion in a poem he wrote to capture the event.

Pictured Left: Paddy and the family in 1959 standing at the base of Governor Walker's pillar on a trip around the Derry Walls on August 12.

82

Governor Walker

In Derry we had a Governor who stood upon the wall
With a guard rail all around him in case that he should fall
'Twas near the end of August in the year of '73
As the pillar was disintegrated the Bogsiders laughed with glee

For there he stood and scorned them for a century and a half
Now is it any wonder that the Bogsiders laughed
The Governor was a symbol of many days of yore
Was from there they burned poor Lundy, but they'll burn him there no more

'Twas heading up for one o'clock most people were in bed
When this terrific explosion all around us could be heard
Some people looked from windows, from doors and wondered why!
The effigy of Governor was no longer in the sky
For down along the Banking, Fahan Street and all around
The fragments of the pillar and parts of Governor could be found

Now don't forget the pillar, and even around the Mem
Is guarded and protected by at least 200 men
They have sentry posts and lookouts and posts of every kind
Well whoever blew the pillar, they don't seem to mind
They scaled upon the Derry Walls to do the job as planned
To leave him lay upon the base without a pillar for a stand
The job was very neatly done for everyone to see
There wasn't even a window broke nor a crib from you or me

Paddy Duffy - August 1973

All was not lost for Governor Walker as the statue itself was rescued and renovated. He now sits in a lowlier, but intact position behind the Memorial Hall in Society Street.

A memorable event which caused a fair bit of craic in November 1977 was the arrival of a whale into the River Foyle, affectionately nicknamed in typical Derry fashion as Dopey Dick.

Dopey Dick in the River Foyle taken by Stuart Arthur in November 1977

Paddy wrote this great poem which described the mood and fun that Dopey's visit had injected across the city.

The Story of Dopey

Into the Foyle's dark waters on a cold November day
A young whale from the ocean by accident did stray
Going past Moville up to Culmore he steered a steady path
Until he reached the Derry Bridge he says 'I'm here at last'

Now nets and buoys and barricades were stretched from shore to shore
With armoured cars and SLR's and soldiers by the score:
'We'll do our duty' was their cry 'of this we cannot fail'
For we made sure that beneath this bridge no one will ever sail

Now when he saw the barriers he said 'I'll not be beat'
This river's wide from shore to shore but in the middle deep
I'll wait until the darkness falls and move up with the tide
And what an awful shock they'll get when I reach the other side

When the news it reached the people about this stranger to their land
They gathered in their thousands and on the bridge and shore did stand
To the City Side and Waterside they came from far and near
And every time he raised his head they gave a mighty cheer

'Twas 'Dopey Dick' they named him for all it was great fun
The Foyle Fisheries and the Army said 'we'll soon have him on the run'
For we have boats and sirens tied up along the quay
And before the day is over he'll be chased back out to sea'

World experts they called in and asked if they could try
To get him to the ocean for if not he'd surely die
But said Dopey 'I don't need them do they think I have no brain!
When I am good and ready I'll go back the way I came'

For near a week we watched him as he frolicked in the Foyle
We thank him for his visit and for the giving us so much joy
Good luck to you brave Dopey on your journeys through the seas
And when you pass Lough Foyle again call in and see us, please."

Paddy Duffy

*A lovely picture of Paddy taken in
August 1982, on the Derry Walls,
enjoying the fresh air and scenery whilst
on the look-out for something to capture
in a sketch or embed into a carving*

Paddy possessed a great retentive memory and recalled many of his favourite poems right up to his death in 1996. One of his favourite poets was Robert W Service (1874 – 1958) whose wit, humour and insight into human behaviour made his poems come to life. He was described as a peoples' poet renowned for his clear, power-packed, dramatic stories. His poems were strongly influenced by his life in Canada and the harshness of the environment, particularly during the gold-rush years.

Very little encouragement was needed for Paddy to recite one of his favourite Robert Service poems, "The Shooting of Dan McGrew." The poem has some very dramatic lines, which Paddy embellished through his deep rasping voice and his timing of the story. Some of the lines in the poem refer to Dan McGrew's love, "the lady that's known as Lou." We always recall with a smile that when it came to that line, Daddy would find his deepest bass voice and would stretch the word "Looouuuuuuu" out as far as he could to increase the drama of the recitation.

The Shooting of Dan McGrew
By Robert W Service

"A bunch of the boys were whooping it up in the Malamute saloon;
The kid that handles the music-box was hitting a rag-time tune;
Back in the bar, in a solo game, sat Dangerous Dan McGrew,
And watching his luck was his light-o'-love, the lady that's known as Lou.

When out of the night, which was fifty below, and into the din and the glare,
There stumbled a miner fresh from the creeks, dog-dirty, and loaded for bear.
He looked like a man with a foot in the grave and scarcely the strength of a louse,
Yet he tilted a poke of dust on the bar, and he called for drinks for the house.
There was none could place the stranger's face, though we searched ourselves
for a clue;
But we drank his health, and the last to drink was Dangerous Dan McGrew.

There's men that somehow just grip your eyes, and hold them hard like a spell;
And such was he, and he looked to me like a man who had lived in hell;
With a face most hair, and the dreary stare of a dog whose day is done,
As he watered the green stuff in his glass, and the drops fell one by one.
Then I got to figuring who he was, and wondering what he'd do,
And I turned my head – and there watching him was the lady that's known as Lou.

His eyes went rubbering round the room, and he seemed in a kind of daze,
Till at last that old piano fell in the way of his wandering gaze.
The rag-time kid was having a drink; there was no one else on a stool,
So the stranger stumbles across the room, and flops down there like a fool.
In a buckskin shirt that was glazed with dirt he sat, and I saw him sway;
Then he clutched the keys with his talon hands – my God but that man could play.

Were you ever out in the Great Alone, when the moon was awful clear,
And the icy mountains hemmed you in with a silence you could not bear;
With only a howl of the timber wolf, and you camped there in the cold,
A half-dead thing in a stark, dead world, clean mad for the muck called gold;
While high overhead, green yellow and red, the North Lights swept in bars? –
Then you've a hunch what the music meant ... hunger and night and the stars.

And the hunger not of the belly kind, that's banished with bacon and beans,
But the gnawing hunger of lonely men for a home and all that it means;
For a fireside far from the cares that are, four walls and a roof above;
But oh! So cramful of cosy joy, and crowned with a woman's love –
A woman dearer than all the world, and true as Heaven is true –
(God! how ghastly she looks through her rouge, – the lady that's known as Lou.)

Then all of a sudden the music changed, so soft that you scarce could hear;
But you felt that your life had been looted clean of all that you once held dear;
That someone had stolen the woman you loved; that her love was a devil's lie;
That your guts were gone, and the best for you was to crawl away and die.
'Twas the crowning cry of a heart's despair, and it thrilled you through and through –
"I guess I'll make it a spread misere," said Dangerous Dan McGrew.

The music almost died away ... then it burst like a pent-up flood;
And it seemed to say, "Repay, repay," and my eyes were blind with blood.
The thought came back of an ancient wrong, and it stung like a frozen lash,
And the lust awoke to kill, to kill ... then the music stopped with a crash,
And the stranger turned, and his eyes they burned in a most peculiar way;
In a buckskin shirt that was glazed with dirt he sat, and I saw him sway;
Then his lips went in, in a kind of grin, and he spoke, and his voice was calm,
And "Boys," says he, "you don't know me, and none of you care a damn;
But I want to state, and my words are straight, and I'll bet my poke they're true,
That one of you is a hound of hell ... and that one is Dan McGrew."

Then I ducked my head, and the lights went out, and two guns blazed in the dark,
And a woman screamed, and the lights went up, and two men lay stiff and stark.
Pitched on his head, and pumped full of lead, was Dangerous Dan McGrew,
While the man from the creeks lay clutched to the breast of the lady that's known as Lou.
These are the simple facts of the case, and I guess I ought to know.
They say that the stranger was crazed with "hooch," and I'm not denying it's so.
I'm not so wise as the lawyer guys, but strictly between us two –
The woman that kissed him and pinched his poke – was the lady that's known as Lou."

Another of Robert Service's poems which Paddy loved was The Cremation of Sam McGee. It has very similar narrative, drama and wit and the following extract may provide a flavour of the rest, it is really worth a read so I won't tell you the ending!

The Cremation of Sam McGee

There are strange things done in the midnight sun by the men who moil for gold;
The Arctic trails have their secret tales that would make your blood run cold;
The Northern Lights have seen queer sights, but the queerest they ever did see
Was that night on the marge of Lake Lebarge I cremated Sam McGee.

Now Sam McGee was from Tennessee, where the cotton blooms and blows.
Why he left his home in the South to roam 'round the Pole,' God only knows.
He was always cold, but the land of gold seemed to hold him like a spell;
Though he'd often say in his homely way that he'd 'sooner live in hell'.

On a Christmas Day we were mushing our way over the Dawson trail.
Talk of your cold! through the parka's fold it stabbed like a driven nail.
If our eyes we'd close, then the lashes froze till sometimes we couldn't see;
It wasn't much fun, but the only one to whimper was Sam McGee.

And that very night, as we lay packed tight in our robes beneath the snow,
And the dogs were fed, and the stars o'erhead were dancing heel and toe,
He turned to me, and "Cap," says he, "I'll cash in this trip, I guess;
And if I do, I'm asking that you won't refuse my last request."

Well, he seemed so low that I couldn't say no; then he says with a sort of moan:
"It's the cursed cold, and it's got right hold till I'm chilled clean through to the bone.
Yet 'tain't being dead -- it's my awful dread of the icy grave that pains;
So I want you to swear that, foul or fair, you'll cremate my last remains."

There's more……. But not here.

In later years Paddy developed severe arthritis in his wrists and ultimately wasn't able to carve or draw. This little poem found in one of his journals expresses his frustration with what used to be the ultimate tools of his trade as a boxer, artist, sculptor and working man - his hands.

For years I used them for work and handicraft
But now as I try to use them it nearly drives me daft
For years I've been treating them with creams and ointment
But when I try to use them I never am content
I used to paint and sketch and draw the scenes around our town
But now I'm discontented and often sit and frown
The things of art that came to me no longer can I do
I cannot even do a job or even draw the 'bru!'

Paddy Duffy

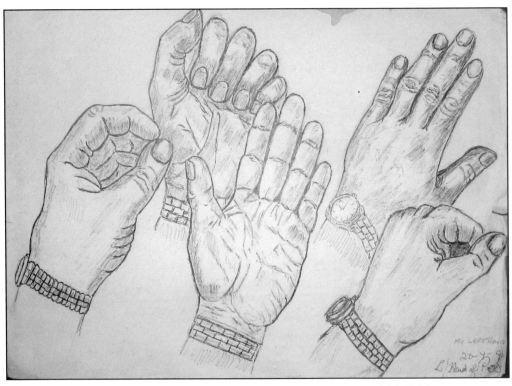

Take these hands . . . . Paddy sketched his left hand 20/7/91

9.   *The Man of Faith*

"I must keep my wits about me, the devil is more cunning than I."

Pope John XX111

In August 1966, at the age of 46, Paddy went on a Joe Walsh Tour to Rome. He had a lifelong ambition to see the works of Michaelangelo and to witness at first hand the wonderful paintings and sculptures that until then had been glimpsed at through a book or on a black & white television.

Michaelangelo di Lodivico Buonarroti was born near Florence, Italy in 1475. He died in 1564 at the age of 89. He was an artist and sculptor of the Renaissance period and his most famous painting was probably the ceiling of the Cistine Chapel. He spent four years from 1509 to 1512 painting the ceiling lying on his back using scaffolding to negotiate across the massive area. His most famous sculpture was the statue of David poised in readiness to fight the giant Goliath. This remarkable piece is made out of marble, stands 16ft – 10 ins tall and is still preserved today. Paddy found it hard to comprehend how someone could have such insight, talent and creativity to create these wonderful works of art that remain today as legacies of the past.

Tour group at the Coliseum, Rome 1966

90

The visit to Rome was a great adventure for Paddy and he can be seen kneeling in front of the Coliseum in the centre of the group wearing a white tee shirt. To his right is Eddie Campbell who has some lucid memories of the trip.

> *"I had known Paddy (Barman) Duffy since my childhood days and laterally in his role as a bouncer at Borderland, the well known dance hall in Muff, Co. Donegal. So I was pleasantly surprised as I boarded the plane in Dublin in 1966 at the age of 22 to fly to Rome (my first ever flight) to see Paddy Duffy and his friend Joe McDonald from Muff seated half-way down the cabin. Also aboard was the well-known Derry businessman Larry Hasson and his late wife Nellie.*
>
> *The flight to Rome was uneventful and made livelier by Paddy's commentary on the many historic sites in Europe which we were flying over. For example, as we crossed the Alps, Paddy would refer to Hannibal and his elephants crossing the Alps centuries before on his way to Rome. I then realised that not only was Paddy a gifted artist, but he was very well read in history from Roman times to the present.*
>
> *We landed briefly in Rimini where some passengers disembarked and new arrivals boarded. I remember Paddy saying jovially 'Buncrana wans this way' to the people getting off.*
>
> *It was around midnight when we flew into Fiumicino airport in Rome and went by bus to our hotel, the Hotel Pegaso (Pegasus) near the city centre. One of the tour representatives was Eugene McGee, brother of Dr. John McGee, now Bishop of Clones and formerly Secretary to three Popes, Pope Paul VI, John Paul I and John Paul II.*
>
> *After a great nights sleep, Paddy, myself and Joe McDonald awoke to our first morning in Rome and sampled the local coffee and ice-cream. Paddy was entranced by the many historic sites and began to sketch those which particularly held his interest. Paddy began to make firm friends with everyone in the group. It seemed as though people were naturally drawn to the quiet, dignified big man from Derry, whose reserve, wit and charm won everybody over. This was especially true of a Parish Priest from Monaghan who was to present Paddy with a set of oil paints and brushes.*

The week progressed with visits to historic sites. As we entered St. Peter's Basilica we heard the sound of singing and saw a group of pilgrims from Spain enter the Basilica on their knees, holding lit candles and singing hymns in Spanish. Paddy said 'What great faith those people have, anybody who didn't believe would be inspired by them.'

It was a beautiful sunny August morning when we travelled to Castelgandolfo, the Pope's summer residence, for a public audience with Pope Paul VI. I remember we were all gathered in the vast Audience Hall and when the Pope entered, there was thunderous cheering and applause. The Pope took his seat, said The Angelus and went on to speak in Italian, French, German and English. The Pope seated on his portable throne, the Seda Gestatoria (Majestic Seat) proceeded slowly down the aisle of the Hall blessing the people left and right and shaking hands. I had a camera and was snapping away as the Pope got closer. Suddenly the Pope turned toward me with his hand outstretched and I let the camera go while I took his hand. Paddy, his eyes full of tears was the first person to shake my hand, as did several other people around me.

I then went off to Rimini on the Adriatic coast and it was during that time that Paddy had the private audience with Pope Paul VI, an event which he carried with him for the rest of his life.

For myself, it was all a great experience to visit Rome but it would not have been so memorable had I not been able to spend so much time in the company of a true Christian gentleman, Paddy Duffy. A man renowned for his wit, his humour, his gentleness, his love of sport especially boxing, and his great love of art and history. But above all of that and before all of that was his love for his Big Bird as he fondly called her, his delightful wife Sadie. Then came his family and after that I truly believed Paddy loved the whole world. Oh yes, and he loved his dogs too, Fido, Rory and Pedro were the three I knew.

To anyone who had done him the slightest favour or courtesy, Paddy would say 'You'll be prayed for at Muff Petty Sessions.' Well I know Paddy that you will be prayed for in far higher courts than that. It was a pleasure and a privilege to have known a man like Paddy. I can only repeat the words of St. Thomas More, another man for all seasons, another man of faith and principle

'Pray for us as we will pray for you until we all meet merrily in heaven.' May his gentle soul rest in peace."

Through a set of mysterious circumstances, which Paddy never did manage to unravel, he was invited to have a private audience with Pope Paul VI. Paddy recalled many times the series of events which led to the invitation from the Vatican and could only speculate why he had been chosen to be honoured in that way.

The tour group that Paddy joined had a public audience with Pope Paul VI at his summer residence planned into the itinerary. There were literally hundreds of people waiting for the Pope to pass by. Paddy managed to get to the front intending to get as close as he could to Pope Paul on his route along the walkway. As the Pope proceeded towards the spot where Paddy was waiting, he spotted an elderly lady behind him in tears, who was too small and frail to find her way to the front of the barrier. Just before the Pope reached him, Paddy stepped back and ushered the lady forward to take his place so that she would have the privileged position. He unselfishly gave up his chance to be close to Pope Paul in order that someone else could benefit. He remembered feeling very emotional being in such close proximity to the Holy Father and was grateful for the opportunity just to be there. The tour group then gathered together and returned to their hotel talking over the experiences of the day.

Later that evening the group met in the foyer of the hotel and a messenger from the Vatican came up to Paddy with an invitation for a private audience with Pope Paul VI the following day. The messenger also carried a red rose, which he also gave to Paddy. As you can imagine, Paddy was absolutely stunned as were the other members of the tour group. The messenger departed and Paddy was left in wonderment. What had he done to deserve this honour? Why was he chosen? How did the messenger know his name? How did he know where to find him? The invitation allowed for Paddy to bring a guest and he offered the place to Majella O'Kane (now deceased), who was also from Derry. She accepted the honour gratefully and on 31st August 1966, they went to the Vatican for the private audience.

The Holy Father spoke to Paddy in English and asked where he was from. Paddy replied that he was from Ireland and the Holy Father commented that it was a very beautiful country. He told Paddy to

"Uphold the faith and if necessary, die for it."

The photograph of the audience in itself tells a wonderful story from the expressions on the faces and offers a sense of the atmosphere of the day. The Cardinal in the centre of the picture was one of Pope Paul's aides.

Paddy shaking hands with Pope Paul VI

Throughout the rest of Paddy's life he consistently pondered why he had been chosen and awarded such an honour. He never did find the answer, however the only link he could surmise that may have been a factor, was his unselfish act in relinquishing his opportunity to be close to the Holy Father at the public audience and allowing an old, frail lady to take his place. His best guess was that this unselfish act was noticed by someone in an official capacity who was empowered to organise the private audience. The mystery of just how he was identified and traced to receive the invitation for the audience remained as it began, an absolute mystery to this day.

The story doesn't end there. As Paddy and Majella exited from the private audience, they were both overwhelmed with emotion and found it hard to absorb what they had just experienced. They were still in the Vatican chambers when an elderly nun approached Paddy and asked if she could talk to him. The nun was Italian and spoke in English. She held Paddy's hands and asked if he would take a relic of the "true cross" back to Ireland and use it to help people in need. She was very forceful in stipulating that Paddy must be the guardian of this relic and that it should never leave his family. The relic was a tiny splinter of wood mounted on a white base and she pressed it into Paddy's hands again asking him to look after it and use it to help others.

Paddy was again overwhelmed and stared in disbelief reflecting all that had happened in such a short space of time. He had met Pope Paul V1 in a private audience and had been bestowed a relic of the "true cross" to take back to Ireland, all in the space of an hour. As you can imagine, Paddy had so many stories to tell on his return and we all remember listening in wonderment and asking all the same questions over and over again *"Daddy, how did the Pope know your name? How did he know what hotel you were staying in? Why did the nun pick you? Why did she give the relic to you?"* Over and over again Paddy also asked himself the same questions and no answers emerged, only speculation and best guesses.

On his return to Derry, Paddy mounted the relic into the body of a gold fob watch case where the section of the true cross can be seen through the glass. Paddy spent a lot of time visiting those who were ill or worried and who requested to hold the relic to provide comfort or as an expression of faith. He spent a lot of time visiting hospitals, hospices and travelling to people in their homes if they requested to visit. The relic remains in the family today and we still continue the work that Daddy began.

The Bullet and The Rosary

Throughout the years of The Troubles in Northern Ireland, Paddy could be regularly seen as a steward on various civil rights and peace marches. His first role as a steward was on The Derry Citizens Action Committee march, which took place on 16th November 1968.

Paddy believed passionately in building harmony, co-operation and acceptance across political and religious divides whilst at the same time providing freedom for individuals and communities to practice their chosen rituals and beliefs.

Bishop Edward Daly recalls memories of Paddy with great respect and affection.

> *"I have a persistent memory of Paddy sitting sketching, often with a group of children or onlookers close by and always with his faithful dog by his side.*
>
> *One enduring memory, which I mentioned in my book, occurred on Bloody Sunday. Paddy was a Steward in the parade and I met him in William Street. I noticed that a group of young boys were behaving mischievously around Chamberlain Street and I asked Paddy to check what they were up to and disperse them. A few moments later the army charged forward and I lost sight of Paddy. I heard later that he had been injured."*

The story picks up from evidence presented at The Bloody Sunday Inquiry. In summary, Paddy and the group of boys he went to disperse were trapped at the bottom of the stairwell of the Rossville Street flats. He and the boys found shelter in a nearby doorway and they were joined by a few others who were unable to find their way through. Paddy and another man acted as 'unofficial doormen' ensuring the children remained inside the doorway. A small British Army Paratrooper with a blackened face challenged Paddy about who was inside the doorway and Paddy responded *"There's no-one in here son, no shooters, just wee 'uns."*

The evidence goes on to describe how the Paratrooper swiftly moved to kick Paddy in the groin and then follow it up with a shot from a rubber bullet gun at point blank range. The rubber bullet hit the top of Paddy's left thigh. The next day Paddy met the same man who had been in the doorway with him and showed him a 9 inch bruise on his left thigh with a distinctive black mark in the middle. Paddy was not angry or bitter about his injuries, in fact he felt that he had been saved by some sort of divine intervention.

"How come.........?" Paddy explained that he had been carrying a metal snuffbox in his left trouser pocket inside which he carried his Rosary Beads. The rubber bullet had hit the snuffbox and this deflected the intensity of the shot at such short range. The box was dented, the Rosary Beads were intact and Paddy had used them on Bloody Sunday to lead the mourners in saying The Rosary over the bodies of some of the victims of that day.

Alec O'Donnell recalls an unforgettable experience as an 18 year old, when Paddy's intervention saved him.........from the wrath of his Ma.

> *"It was back in 1970 and I was at a Civil Rights March or a peace march of some sort. More often than not there was trouble at these gatherings – marches and riots in those days often went hand in hand.*
>
> *The march was going down Great James Street and up past Victoria Market heading towards the Guildhall. We were chanting 'We shall overcome.' After the meeting most of the crowd dispersed and then there was an attack on the Victoria Barracks and a battle between the British Army and rioters started.*
>
> *During this stage of The Troubles there were men like Barman Duffy and Vinny Coyle, along with priests and people like John Hume who tried to act as stewards and head off any violence. A riot broke out and we were pushed back to William Street by Littlewoods corner. Barman Duffy and Vinny Coyle were trying to keep things under control. At this time the Army had developed new units called 'snatch squads.' As the name suggests, these units consisted of*

soldiers who came into crowds and literally snatched people in the front line. A 'snatch squad' was released at Littlewoods corner and I remember trying to make my way back to The Bog. I remember running as fast as I could but some one in front of me tripped, then I tripped and a big Brit got hold of me. He grabbed me by the scruff of my neck and I couldn't shake him off.

I remember thinking 'That's it, they'll drag me to the barracks, I'll get a hiding, then I'll be up in front of Judge Paddy Maxwell in court in the morning and I'll be put away for six months.' All of that I could handle........... My instant panic was telling my Ma. I didn't want my mother to think I was down the town rioting – she would have killed me.

As this young Brit was dragging me away I noticed Barman Duffy coming towards us slowly with his arms outstretched. As he came near I grabbed him by the lapels of his coat and wasn't letting go. I pleaded with him 'Barman don't let them take me away, me Ma'll kill me!' Barman calmly talked to the Brit, he kept saying things like 'Leave the young fella alone, sure he wasn't even involved, let that boy go home to his mother.' He kept on talking calmly to the Brit and whatever influence his presence had, the young soldier let me go. At that Barman turned to me and said 'Run, run like hell to your mother' and I did. I ran all the way home."

Throughout his life, Paddy made at least twenty pilgrimages to Lough Derg, often referred to as Saint Patrick's Purgatory. Lough Derg lies about four miles north of the village of Pettigo in County Donegal. It is described as a special place of peace and personal challenge and has been receiving pilgrims continuously for well over 1000 years.

Nowadays there are a variety of different types of pilgrimages to Lough Derg and Paddy always undertook the three day traditional pilgrimage which consists of a three day Pilgrimage Fast and Pilgrimage Exercises undertaken in bare feet. Pilgrims arrive on the island between 11:00am and 3:00pm on the first day, having fasted from midnight.

The Pilgrimage Exercises are made up of a prayer sequence called a "Station". This is a well-known Celtic form of prayer, involving physical movement accompanied by 'mantra type' prayers. Nine Stations are completed on Lough Derg over the three day period. Five Stations are made on in the open air on the 'Penitential Beds' while pilgrims say the prayers of Four Stations together in the Basilica.

The central penitential exercise of the Pilgrimage is the Vigil; each pilgrim stays

Morning and Evening Mass is celebrated in St. Patrick's Basilica each day as well as other liturgies throughout the second day of pilgrimage when there is also time for personal reflection. Pilgrims have one "Lough Derg Meal" of dry toast or oatcake and black tea or coffee on each of the three days of the Pilgrimage.

In earlier times the area around the lake was a place of protection for anyone in trouble. The monastery nearby offered hospitality to all. Today Lough Derg still reaches out to those in need. Whatever their creed, background, social circumstances or religious practice, all are made welcome.

The philosophy underpinning the Lough Derg experience is that :

> *"There are no outsiders here: in bare feet, everyone is equal. Pilgrims journey together: they share each other's joy, feel each other's pain. We try to ensure that everyone's story is heard and that help is offered for the continuing journey of life."*

10. *The Collector*

"Don't throw away the old bucket until you know whether
the new one holds water."

Swedish Proverb

Paddy was an avid collector of ……...pretty much everything. He was probably the equivalent of a modern day ecologist as he could see value, reusable potential and often beauty in many of the things that most people discarded. He would collect all sorts of stuff ; odd bits of wood for carvings e.g. banisters, snooker cues, Christmas trees; unusually shaped stones and vegetables; the foil trays that tarts were baked in. He would mould these around coins and ornaments to create a fresh mould with new textures and finishes etc. etc. Every now and then Mum would complain that the house was looking like "Nellie Ramsay's" and would have a clear-out raid.

Derry Nicknames
One of Paddy's more "tidy" collectables was a series of little notebooks in which he recorded a host of anecdotes, sayings, quotations, poems, witticisms and one of his favourite topics, Derry nicknames. His own nickname "Barman" was coined when he started working in a bar in his late teens. He was always fascinated by the way nicknames developed and then were perpetuated to become a part of a common language across the city. Most people were aware of their nicknames and accepted them with good humour and grace. There were however some who were not aware or, who were not at all happy with the them.

The wit and humour behind the nicknames intrigued Paddy and I've included the complete list of 448 Derry nicknames he collected in one of his journals. Apologies in advance if anyone reading this falls into the latter category of people who were unhappy with their nickname.

A

100 Doherty
14 Duffy
71 Gallagher
Admiral Doherty
Ambrose Moore
Andy the Blower Doherty
Anney Doot Rogers
Arsey Pat
Artie Orr
Ass In Pockets

B

Backett Cartin
Bacon McCready
Baldy White
Bamm Nicell
Banks McMenamin
Banty Gallagher
Banty Lewis
Barman Duffy
Beasie Bullseye
Beatle Cunningham
Beatley McBride
Bedo McCallion
Bella the Dead
Belshaw Doherty
Big Dan Harkin
Big Joe Hunter
Big Paddy McGilloway
Billy the Liar McFeely
Bing Roddy
Black Barney Doherty
Black Charlie McLaughlin
Blanket King
Blister Burns
Blue Smith
Bogside Paddy Doherty

B

Boob Wallace
Boots McDaid
Bottle Pint
Bradban Curran
Briddley Kane
Brinny Egg Doherty
Brock Carlin
Broken Nose Campbell
Buck McGeady
Buck Sharkey
Budgem Callaghan
Budgem Doherty
Buff Meenan
Bugs Doherty
Bull Campbell
Bungalow Doherty
Bunker Kelly
Bunty McGinley
Bus Meenan
Busty Coyle
Busty Smith
Busty McGowan
Butt End Duffy
Butcher Flemming

C

Cab Devine
Caker Casey
Cannibal Bonner
Carton Duffy
Chalk A Water Gallagher
Champer Hegarty
Chang Gallagher
Change the Yank
Charlie the Hill Man
Charlie the Whistler Smith

C

Cheapy McLaughlin
Chesty Crossan
Chesty Nicholl
Chopgha Faulkner
Chum Carson
Chummy Keys
Conna Brown
Cooter Quigley
Copper Mouth Doherty
Corky Doran
Country Duffy
Crack McLaughlin
Crow Kelly
Crusty Quinn
Curly Bella Campbell
Cush Nash
Cushey Haslett

D

Da Little
Da Willie McLaughlin
Dadhler Cusack
Dan the Liar Nash
Dan the Rag
Danny Glut Doherty
Darkie Dinny McLaughlin
Dead Level
Dead Man Riley
Dead Pan Nicholl
Dido Keys
Digger Barr
Digger Quigley
Din Tracey
Dip Connor
Dirty Dick McLaughlin
Dirty Feet
Dixie Travers

D

Dock Doherty
Dom O'Donnell
Doodle Tracey
Doodles McCallion
Dot Duddy
Dotsey Coyle
Dottie Doherty
Double Doherty
Douce Clifford
Doughball Bradley
Drakie Tracey
Drooling Johnson
Drum Major
Duck Egg
Ducky Burkey
Duke Da Gillespie
Duke Doran

E

Eddie the Dead
Effie Bonner
Egg O'Donnell
Elkie Clark

F

F Maguire (Ring the Bell)
Fagan Kelly(Miser)
Fanny James Smith
Farmer McGeehan
Fat Harkin
Fay Coyle
Fiddler O'Donnell
Fintown Ghost McCloskey
Fisty Doyle
Fisty Muldoon

F

Flitty Dalton
Flucky Mc Dermott
Fly Doherty
Friday Kane
Fudgie McGuire
Fusell Kelly

G

Gacky McFadden
Gaggy McAnny
Gander Scanlon
German Canning
Ghosty Dohert
Ginky Harkin
Gleek Doherty
Glig Brown
Gludger Friel
God Duffy
Gooldie McAteer
Gorder Scanlon
Granda McGlinchey
Grazey Mickie
Grazey Creswell
Grey Man Doherty
GripperMeenan
Gulldag Doherty
Gulpin Sharkey
Gunner McCallion
Gurkey Gallagher
Gutsy McGonagle

H

Hagan Barr
Half a Loaf
Hang Daw
Harbour Master Gallagher
Harry Treacle Doherty
Harry Waste
Hawk Duffy
Hawker Lynch
Heavy McAllister
Hendaw Burns
Hen Henderson
Hen McGinley
Hookie Fleming
Hookey Moore
Hookey Nicholl
Hootsie Hargan
Horsey Doran
Horsey Wade
Hughie Slack McLaughlin
Hughie the Geek McCloskey
Hughie the Gleek
Hump Campbell

I

Inky Bonner
Inky Coyle

J

Jane The Goat
Jimbo Crossan
Jimbo Curran
Jimmy The Man
Jobby Crossan
Jock Smith
Joe The Caddy
Johnny Coyle
Johnny Blue McGuinness

J

Johnny Cuttems
Johnny Raw
Johnny Sabuck
John TheNarrowmanMcLaughlin
Johnny the German
Jooker Doughie

K

Kid Barlow
Kid Caufield
Kid Donnnelly
K Paddy McCloskey
King McLaughlin
Kitty the Hare
Knowledge O'Donnell
K Paddy McCloskey

L

Lady Dixon
Lancer Doherty
Large Stewart
Lark O'Donnell
Leah Shan Doherty
Leg McCourt
Leggy Ferguson
Long Toes Friel
Lovely Dan McLaughlin
Lovely Quinn
Lumber O'Neil

M

Mad Dog Doherty
Maggie McCay
Magwa Campbell
Mak a Wing
Marcus Himself Harrison
Marky McLaughlin
Marrow Boyle
Mary the Cat
Mausie Caufield
Maxie Devine
Maxie Mulhern
Mickie Fish
Midge Blakely
Midge Kelly
Midge Mc Garrigle
Midge Rankin
Mighty Breslin
Miser McConnell
Mitcham McLaughlin
Molly of the Moor
Monkey Moore
Monkey Nash
Monkey O'Brien
Mousie Brady
Mucka McDermott
Mutt Smith
My Ma Hart

N

Nag McFadden
Nags Hegarty
Namer Ross
Narrow Man McLaughlin
Neck Hasson
Neil Pig Egg O'Donnell

N

Nigger McLaughlin
Nine Jaws Biddy
Nobby Carr
Nobby Clark
Nobby Lynch
Noggy Brown
Nugger Smith

O

Oakey Ramsay
One Glass McLaughlin
Onion Cassidy

P

Pa McGuinness
Pacer Ferguson
Packets McGilloway
Paddy Brogan Doherty
Paddy Coke
Paddy Hard Times
Paddy McGinty Long
Paddy My Ass Duffy
Paddy Shan Doherty
Paddy the Buck Mc Callion
Paddy the Hab
Paddy the Saxton
Paddy the Stall
Paper Kite Friel

P

Peach Campbell
Peggy Strain
Pepper Doherty
Perch Roach
Peter the Saddler
Phil Lizzie Harkin
Pickett Mc Laughlin
Piggy McClintock
Piggy Melaugh
Pin Head Kinnear
Pin McCloskey
Piper Cassidy
PJ Kelly
Pod Doherty
Pope Gallagher
Pope Leo McCauley
Porgy Wallace
Porky Green
Potter Canning
Potter Mullan
Poundies McCready
Puddy Campbell
Pussy Hegarty
Pussy Patterson
Putty Campbell

R

Rab Simpson
Ranger Harkin
Rattler Deehan
Red Barney Doherty
Red Joe O'Donnell
Red Willie Doherty
Rickety Walker
Robert the Bird

Rosie Tyrone
Rubber Nose
Roper O'Donnell
Runty Cochrane
Ruthan Mc Laughlin

S

Saddler McLaughlin
Salmon Culhoun
Sam Dung
Scase Gibbons
Scone Callan
Scott Dan Doherty
Scout Robinson
Scrub McLaughlin
Shafter Bradley
Shavas Logue
Sheriff Platt
Shifty Meenan
Shooey Gallagher
Shoot Deehan
Shudley Gallagher
Silly Bugles Johnson
Skelper Doherty
Skin Divin
Skin McCartney
Skinner Harvey
Skinny Harkin
Slabber Doherty
Slabbery Mickey
Slater Doherty
Slim Keegan
Smokey Rodgers
Snag Carroll
Snake Eye McCafferty
Snib Donaghey

S

Snig Bradley
Snig Kelly
Snigger Doherty
Snigger Smith
Snout Doherty
Snow Mc Colgan
Snowy Johnson
Snowy Shannon
Soldier Campbell
Sonny Doherty
Sonny Mackay
Sparrow Lyttle
Speedy McCafferty
Spider Kelly
Spider McElhinney
Spider Scanlon
Spike Elliott
Spittle Doherty
SpoonMcShane
Sprig McCauley
Sprig McCrystal
Spud Murphy
Squire Devenney
Squire Nellis
Stacey Pat Friel
Stall Doherty
Star Coyle
Steely Cassidy
Stewbag McFadden
Sticky Sheerin
Stiff Nash
Stinker O'Neil
Stocky McCallion
Stovey Bradley
Stovey Martin
Stovie McClelland
Stracka Doherty
String Doherty

S

Sucker McIntyre
Sugar Ray Pickett
Sunshine Doyle
Switcher Harkin

T

Ta Simms
Ta Tracey
Tammy O'Connnell
Tanty Howard
Taper Cassidy
Tartles Mc Cafferty
Tarzan Canney
Tarzan McCallion
Tasty McLaughlin
Teamy Alan
Teamy Dolan
The Greek Doherty
The Saxton Sharkey
The Turn McLaughlin
Thunderbolt Devlin
Tasty McLaughlin
Tibbs Harkin
Tie the Body
Time Enough
Time Enough Doherty
Tin McCloskey
Tipperary Canavan (Captain)
Titty Doherty
Toby McFeely
Toddler Gallagher
Tom Daisy
Tommy Tit Faulkner
Ton Deehan

T

Toots Curran
Tossey Thomas 11
Tots Mc Dermott
Towie Friel
Treacle Doherty
Tucker Smith
Twin Doherty

W

Wallop Monteith
Wan Wing Bradley
Wang Doherty
Wang Mc Cann
Warpy Edwards
Wart Mc Callion
Watchey Barratt
Whaler Gillespie
Whiskers Lafferty
Wiggy McGuinness
Willie Belfast McLaughlin
Willie the Devil
Windmill Doherty
Winker Kelly
Winkle Doherty
Winkle Mooney
Winkle Smith
Wire Cullen
Witchie Barrett

Y

Yachts McDermott
Yanty Coyle
Yellow Ned
Yorky Woods
Yunkey McEvoy

Sayings and Anecdotes

Paddy loved witty, mischievous anecdotes and catchphrases and collected many of them in his journals. He was also a very deep thinker earning him the reputation as a philosopher. He collected a range of maxims and sayings which held special meaning for him and which reflected his beliefs and attitudes about life. The name of the person who originated the saying is included where it is known, otherwise the source is unknown.

"Genius may have its limitations, but stupidity is not thus handicapped."

"If there are no stupid questions, then what kind of questions do stupid people ask? Do they get smart just in time to ask questions?"

Scott Adams

"Ordinarily he was insane, but he had lucid moments when he was merely stupid."

"Freedom is not worth anything if it does not include the freedom to make mistakes."

"He who steals my purse steals trash, but he who takes away from me my good name considers himself not, but leaves me poor indeed."

"If a well spent day brings happy sleep, so life well used brings happy death."

"Laugh your head off today, it will be yesterday tomorrow."

"Never explain - your friends don't need it and your enemies won't believe you anyway."

"A want of care does more damage than a want of knowledge."

Q. "What do you put in the corner and it never moves, but it can go to any country in the world?"
A. "A stamp."

"When a thing is funny, search it carefully for a hidden truth."

"Artificial intelligence is not a match for natural stupidity."

This following verse written in one of his journals expressed his view of the world and he would frequently recite it to us. As children, we didn't really appreciate what it really meant and it's only in later life that we've been able to look back and begin to comprehend just what he was trying to teach us.

Take Time

"Take time to pray, it is the greatest power on earth

Take time to think, it is the source of power

Take time to play, it is the secret of perpetual youth

Take time to love and be loved, it is a God-given privilege

Take time to be friendly, it is the road to happiness

Take time to laugh, it is the music of the soul

Take time to give, it is too short a day to be selfish

Take time to work, it is the price of success."

Unknown

11. The Community Man

"If you have much - give your wealth, if you have little - give your heart."

Unknown

Paddy was always keen to support and contribute to community events. In this picture of a Gulliver's Travels Parade, he can be seen posing as a strong man on a float as part of the Long Tower Carnival in 1956/7. At the front of the picture, the little boy and little girl are dressed as a groom and bride. We believe that the central theme of the parade was designed to celebrate the work of Jonathan Swift, the author of Gulliver's Travels.

Gulliver's Travels Parade

Swift was born in Dublin in 1667 and graduated from Trinity College, Dublin in 1692 with a BA and an MA. He was ordained into the Church of Ireland (Anglican) and led a very full life mixing roles in the church, politics, teaching and writing. One of his most famous works was Gulliver's Travels which was published in 1726. Although superficially a children's story, it actually exposed some very profound beliefs and concerns about human behaviour. Swift wrote the book with a serious purpose - "to mend the world." Gulliver's Travels was a topical social satire, a work of propaganda, in which he wanted to show the consequences of humanity's refusal to be reasonable. Swift died in Dublin in 1745 and ironically, many of the themes he explored are still alive and relevant today.

On 9th June 1974, Paddy can be seen on the left of the picture wearing a sash and acting as a steward for a parade to celebrate the collaboration of all Derry Parishes, which was led by the Bishop and the Mayor. The picture was taken in the Brandywell with the Lady of Lourdes Hall in the background.

Derry Parishes Parade 1974

In later years, Paddy was a true community activist getting involved in various organisations and groups aimed at improving the lives of local people across all religious, political and social divides.

One such body was the Maiden City Boxing Association established by bringing together a group of well known ex-boxers, businessmen and others with a genuine concern for the youth of the city. The Chairman was Leo Deehan and Paddy was the vice-chairman. The remit of the Association was summed up in a statement from them:

> *"The club is open to all creeds, both young and old in all walks of life. We have in our midst the future stars of sport and these people may not be given a proper chance. The Maiden City Boxing Association hopes to give them that chance."*

No doubt the motivation to want to help young people to excel and be the best they could be in the sporting context was driven by the personal experiences of all the ex-boxers in the group.

The Maiden City Boxing Association *Front row from the left ; Anthony McGowan, Len Donnelly (Secretary), Leo Deehan (Chairman), Dan Canning, Joe McCallion*
Back row from the left : Frank McConnellogue, Jackie Bonner. Colum McGill (Press Officer), Billy Gallagher, Paddy Duffy (Vice-chairman) Johnny Kennedy, Jim McDaid, Willie McCallion

Dove House

Paddy was also the Vice-Chairman of Dove House when it was originally opened as a Community Resource Centre on 15th November 1984. He conducted the opening ceremony which included a presentation to a visiting Member of the European Parliament (MEP), Mr. Herman Verbeek. To commemorate the occasion, Paddy carved a plaque inserted with a wooden cross which was presented to Mr. Verbeek at the opening ceremony.

Presentation to the MEP Mr. Herman Verbeek on the opening of Dove House

Frankie McMenamin was a Management Committee member and local resident and recalls some fond recollections of working with Paddy on the Dove House project.

"Paddy Barman Duffy got involved in the Dove House Community Resource Centre in November 1984 when myself and Mary Nellis asked him if he would conduct the official opening ceremony. Paddy continued to be actively involved and served as a member of the Management Committee for a further eight years. During that period he served as the Chair for several periods and was instrumental in establishing the management and direction of the project during that era.

To me, Paddy was gentleman, very kind and very direct. The thing that stands out in my mind was his voice - it was very deep yet gentle and had a hypnotic quality. I used to marvel at how big his hands were - they were like shovels. I do remember the love he had for the people he met from anywhere. He had no time for any type of sectarianism or bigtory and he especially loved the people within his community.

I remember Paddy from when I was about eight years old and used to follow him around the town as he would sketch and draw and capture his love of the city in his artwork. All the children were fascinated by him, he was like the Granda everyone would love to have had."

Pilots Row

One of Paddy's great loves in later life was playing bowls. He was a member of the Pilots Row Youth and Community Centre in Rosville Street and played for their Bowls team. He was very proud of the achievements of the team and enjoyed displaying the various cups, trophies and medals they had won. The Centre was also a great place for the community to gather and interact with a common purpose and he enjoyed the exchange of banter and local gossip.

This is going exactly where I want it to!

Paddy can be seen third from left at the back with his arm around Johnny Coyle on his right (now deceased)

Pictured Above: Key organising members of the Pilots Row committee
Left to right: Tommy Harrigan, Paddy Logue, Jim Doherty, Johnny Coyle and Paddy

Paddy in full flow during a presentation at Pilots Row with Paddy Logue in the background. Of course he could always have been reciting "The Shooting of Dan Mc Grew!"

Eddie Campbell has some further memories of Paddy

"In his later years I would always join Paddy sitting on a wall in Rossville Street either sketching or just resting his 'old pins' as he would call his legs.

On several occasions when The Troubles were coming to an end we would encounter foreign visitors, Spanish, Norwegian, Portugese, you name it. Paddy would always chat to them about Derry, its history, its people and would give them directions to where they wanted to go. Invariably they would take our photographs and I would say 'We're all over Europe now Barman.' Paddy would often say 'Should we be getting a grant from the Council for all our work for the tourist trade?"

Earlier in the book I mentioned that our house was always full of pets, waifs and strays. Many of the local people and visitors that Daddy encountered while he was out sketching would be invited back for their tea or dinner. He was so proud of Derry and loved to be able to communicate this to people from all over the world who visited the city. Mum had a built-in contingency plan. She always cooked more food than the family would need as there were usually new faces around the table to entertain. It was also a great opportunity for Daddy to "impress" visitors with his stylophone – that's were we all exited and left many a poor visitor politely enduring the strains of *"a noise like a burst bagpipe invaded by a gang of angry wasps"* loosely playing the tune of Danny Boy!

12. The Final Round

"Stop stranger stop and cast an eye
As you are now so once was I
As I am now so you must be
Prepare for death and follow me."

Unknown

As his general health deteriorated, Daddy was obviously frustrated by the limitations it imposed on his mobility and dexterity. He wrote the following short poem when he was in hospital recovering from a particularly bad episode of congestive cardiac failure. We were so pleased when he did write it because it was a sign that he was getting better and was looking for inspiration from the world around him, which at that point in time was Altnagelvin Hospital.

Into hospital I was taken
With several complaints and no mistaken
The nurses there did treat me good
They really kept me in good mood
They treated all my aches and pains
Even the doctors sucked my veins
To take blood samples for the test
To try to keep me at my best
My legs swelled up twice their size
And really caught me with surprise
For it has taken months to nurse them down
And walking really caused me to frown

Paddy Duffy

When his aches, pains and general health would allow, he used to walk down to Waterloo Place to call into the Post Office to collect his pension. He used to find his way to a small room leading to the entrance of the Northern Counties Hotel. This was a meeting place for a small group of pals who would share a drink; enjoy the craic; talk about each others aches and pains; who had died; who was close to death; the latest jokes; witticisms and no doubt many other topics of the day.

Another meeting place where he enjoyed the craic and an occasional drink was in Tinney's Bar, Patrick Street. The photograph taken in Waterloo Place is still on the wall there along with a small verse that Paddy wrote for his friends in the Bar.

One man and his dog

T   is for the thirst that overcomes me
I   is for the intelligence received
N   is for the nice company that drink there
N   is for the never bad tempered friends there
E   is for the ever pleasant people that go there
Y   is for the years of pleasure spent there

On his journey to Waterloo Place Daddy would meet and greet many people on the way and would stop for a yarn. Mum never knew when to expect him back, it depended on how many people he met on the way and the amount of news and craic there was to exchange.

Daddy's general health deteriorated badly and he passed away peacefully at home on Monday 8th January 1996 at the age of 76. The entire family had been together for Christmas and the New Year and shared some really happy memories, Daddy even managed to get in a verse or two of "The Shooting of Dan McGrew."

The ex-servicemen of the Oglaigh Naisiunta Na hEireann from the Irish Army formed a guard of honour alongside his tricolour-draped coffin on the day of his funeral. We all remember the sound of the lone piper as he led the funeral cortege into The Cemetery and the eerie lament that clung to the cold, crisp air of that January day.

Paddy's funeral, 10th January 1996.

His faithful friend Pedro the Third, just gave up. He stopped eating and drinking and died exactly a week later. Numerous visits to the vet didn't unearth any underlying health problems and his demise was put down to "a broken heart" following the death of his master.

A lot of people who knew Daddy personally, or knew of him, still speak fondly of him and capture their thoughts in phrases like "he was a great man," "he had a real presence," "the most diplomatic and peace- loving man I ever met" "an absolute gentleman" and many more accolades besides. This tribute from Joe Mac Carthy sums up so eloquently the thoughts of so many people whose lives he touched.

Patrick Barman Duffy, Soldier, Poet and Artist

> *"Diplomacy is a word often used when referring to Barman. Dialogue was how he resolved confrontation. As we now enter a new era in our history, it is interesting to note that two things have come to the fore in the lead up to, and subsequent events following, the Peace Process. Diplomacy and dialogue have got us to where we are today. Barman practiced both throughout his life. The real pity is that so many others were blinded by a hate that could only be defeated through diplomacy and dialogue. We are all enriched by the legacy of Barman Duffy through his: poetry, art and carvings. We would do well to practice what he preached and settle future conflicts by plain informed speaking and a caring mindset to all who seek conflict. Perhaps this is Barman's greatest legacy of all."*

To close this book we've chosen an entry from one of Daddy's journals. The words and the sentiments express exactly how he viewed the world, and how he chose to live his life and bring up his family. We miss him and are so grateful for the memories and legacies he has left with us.

"Don'ts

Do not return evil for evil, nothing is achieved by retaliation

Do not judge your brother, leave judgement to God

Do not worry about food or clothes, make it your first concern to live worthy of God

Do not store up treasures for yourself here on earth, money, property,

goods etc. these are like chaff in the eyes of God

Do not give up hope even when times are rough and friends are not to be found

Do's

Love your enemies, that's hard but it will make you special, the very salt of the earth

Give and you will receive in abundance

Forgive your brother when he sins against you, forgive him not just in words but from the heart

Finally, the Commandment that sums it all up ;

* Love one another the way I loved you

* If you do this you are not just my servants, you are my friends"

Unknown

The End

This is a real, true and from-the-heart account of the life of an ordinary man who achieved extraordinary things. Paddy "Barman" Duffy was a man for all seasons who was hired out from a Hiring Fair as a young teenager and went on to develop amazing talents, which on the surface seem contradictory. How could a professional boxer also be an accomplished artist, sculptor, poet, diplomat and family man?

This book has been written by us, his family and tells his story in our own words. We hope that it will inform and inspire others to achieve some things they believe may be unachievable. All profits its sale will be shared with the Foyle Hospice and Foyleview School. Even after his death, his life story will help others. That's the legacy he would want to leave.

Thank you, and as Daddy would have said *"You'll be prayed for at Muff Petty Sessions."*

Sadie Duffy and the Duffy Family

The last photograph taken of Daddy outside The Cardbox in Waterloo Place in November 1995. His faithful friend in the photograph was Pedro the Third, not to be mistaken for Pedro the First and Second who looked exactly the same.